At the Corner of Mundane and Grace

Other books by Chris Fabry

The H.I.M. Book

Spiritually Correct Bedtime Stories

Away with the Manger

The 77 Habits of Highly Ineffective Christians

At the

Finding

Corner of

Glimpses of Glory

Mundane

in Ordinary Days

and Grace

CHRIS FABRY

WATERBROOK
PRESS

AT THE CORNER OF MUNDANE AND GRACE
PUBLISHED BY WATERBROOK PRESS
5446 North Academy Boulevard, Suite 200
Colorado Springs, Colorado 80918
A division of Random House, Inc.

Scripture taken from the *Holy Bible, New International Version*®. NIV®
Copyright © 1973, 1978, 1984 by International Bible Society. Used
by permission of Zondervan Publishing House. All rights reserved.

ISBN 1-57856-117-5

Contact the author by e-mail: Cfabry@compuserve.com

Published in association with the literary agency of Alive Communications, Inc.,
1465 Kelly Johnson Blvd.; Suite 320, Colorado Springs, Colorado 80920

Library of Congress Cataloguing in Publication Data
Fabry, Chris, 1961–
    At the corner of mundane and grace : finding glimpses of glory in
ordinary days / Chris Fabry. — 1st ed.
        p. cm.
    ISBN 1-57856-117-5
    1. Christian life.   I. Title.
BV4501.2.F266   1999
242—dc21   99-14485
                                                                  CIP

Printed in the United States of America
1999—First Edition

10   9   8   7   6   5   4   3   2   1

For my father,
whose hands
I can
still feel
supporting
me

CONTENTS

FOREWORD

by Phillip Gulley

------◆------

When I was in the fifth grade, I won second prize in the Danville Optimist's Bicycle Safety Rodeo. I got ten dollars and a Salisbury-steak dinner at the Westwood Inn next to Johnston's Regal Grocery. My picture appeared in the newspaper alongside Ricky White, the first-place winner, who received a new bike from Floyd's Bicycle Mart. Ricky's father was the president of the Optimist Club, something I found suspicious at the time (and still do).

Winning second place was the biggest honor of my life—up until I was asked to write this foreword. What a privilege!

I have a confession to make. I kept reading *At the Corner of Mundane and Grace* because it made me laugh. That's not a bad thing. There are a host of books that not only won't make you laugh, they won't teach you anything either. That is a serious defect, a book that is both boring and unhelpful. Chris Fabry's book is neither. Long after the laughter faded, the lesson stayed. I learned, just a little bit better, how to recognize God's refreshing presence in the ordinary moments of life.

A big problem in our Christian faith is that we think God is with us only in the pew, when we're spit-shined and all tucked in. Chris Fabry tells us otherwise—that God is with us when we're elbow deep in dirty diapers, when our marriages are faltering, when the kids are sick and the dog is dying. I don't know about you, but I need to learn more about a God like that. I have the stained-glass God all figured out. It's the God of the "everyday" I seek, the God of spilt milk and spilled tears I need to know. Chris Fabry has helped me find Him.

There is a tendency these days to dismiss those truths conveyed through humor, as if people who make us laugh can't also make us think and help us grow. As if that which tickles our funny bones can't also stir our souls. I invite you right now to turn to chapter 8, "A Prayer for Every Day," and read it. Now see if amidst your laughter is found also the "Amen," the "Yes, that's true," the "Lord, make me like that too."

In *At the Corner of Mundane and Grace*, Chris Fabry confirms and celebrates a simple gospel truth—that faith in God brings light and joy to every darkened corner. In this world of dark corners, this is the best news indeed.

I hope you enjoy Chris Fabry's latest offering as much as I have.

I hope that, as you read it, the Christ who is our Joy turns your mourning into dancing.

I hope Chris Fabry keeps on writing.

I hope Ricky White enjoyed his new bicycle.

Foreword

Most important, I hope the God of your Sunday morning becomes the God of your everyday.

—Philip Gulley

Author of *Front Porch Tales, Home Town Tales,* and *For Everything a Season*

Cloud Holding 101

Triumph and tragedy. The world is filled with it every day, and here you stand making lunch or trying to pick up the Sunday paper without getting a hernia. While others reach pinnacles or fall to the depths, you experience blah. It's just another humdrum day.

Or is it?

Could you be missing something important?

I believe heroic faith is forged in everyday furnaces. I believe extraordinary things happen to people who find glimpses of glory in ordinary days.

But when I'm in the middle of grocery lines and traffic, diapers and laundry (not that I do laundry; I tend to watch it pile up), God seems distant and unaware. Am I missing him amid my daily duties? Is there some cosmic lesson I'm overlooking? Should I go with the Rice Krispies treats or the Fruit Roll-Ups for the soccer team's snack today?

If you've been yearning for more of God, this book is for you. If you look closely, you might find he's already given more than you're ready to take.

We've forgotten we serve the God of the humdrum, the Deity who takes a mediocre existence and transforms it into a chorus of praise. The subtle message sent by many books and seminars is that he is only the God of the big splash, the dramatic testimony, the miraculous healing. He is the God who fixes us in one weekend. Don't get me wrong. God does miracles. But he's also King of the Common. Sometimes he chooses not to fix the brokenness of our lives for a reason, and it's in the long haul, these fallow times, that we grow or stagnate.

I want to grow—don't you? Then step into the everyday furnace with me.

My God was a carpenter's son with calluses to prove it. He swept sawdust from the floor at the end of the day. His feet were dirty most of his life. He wiped the sweat from his brow in his Nazareth existence, and for thirty years he waited. He obeyed. He was faithful in the mundane.

We don't hear much about this part of Jesus' life. There aren't many verses dedicated to it, so we concentrate on the big events: the incarnation, the healings, his crucifixion and resurrection. But Jesus was not just biding time on his journey through the ordinary. God had an eternal purpose for the dust and troubles that prepared Jesus for the path of suffering ahead. I believe he has a purpose for the dust you and I encounter today.

In part 1 of this book you'll discover exactly what I mean by mundane. You'll walk through my neighborhood, take a good look at some of my foibles and at the people who have helped me grow, hear some honest confessions, and, I hope, see yourself. In part 2 you'll see how God can take the dismal forecast you're experiencing today and turn it into a divine appointment. It will help you choose the path that leads to joy and true fulfillment.

As you read, I hope you experience the sensation of a gentle hand slipping onto your shoulder, like a father and his child. At other points I want you to feel what I felt when my Uncle Willy hugged me and the people with supplemental oxygen showed up. Each time you open this book, I pray you sense God creeping up on your busy life. I sense this when I look deeply into my children's eyes or when I step in front of a moving bus. It only takes a second to shift your focus to the important things.

Living fully in the ordinary is difficult. It's a little like trying to hold a cloud. As we grasp at distractions, time slips through our fingers. Sometimes it's just easier to let it go and turn on the television. But don't give up. Keep looking, and God will take you by surprise with glimpses of his glory. As you read this book, you might also encounter a few painful self-portraits. Glory is wonderful, but it always shines a light on our flaws.

Whatever this light reveals, take life's ordinary moments and realize they are directly from the Giver of all good things. Doing so will take daily effort. It will stretch your faith *and* your

3

lower back. But your life will be much richer when you open your eyes, seize the gift of "today," and experience it in all its fullness.

God may show up miraculously in your kitchen or on your way to work. Please call if he does. But I bet he'll show himself to you in much smaller ways. Come with me now and renew your spiritual senses. Open your eyes and discover the God who makes his home at the corner of Mundane and Grace.

Part One

At the Corner of Mundane and Grace

The test of the spiritual life is the power to
descend.... We are built for the valley, for
the ordinary stuff we are in, and that is where
we have to prove our mettle.

OSWALD CHAMBERS

Believe me, every man has his secret sorrows,
which the world knows not; and ofttimes we
call a man cold, when he is only sad.

HENRY W. LONGFELLOW

CHAPTER ONE

———❖———

Grace in the Suds

It was one of those lazy summer days you dream about in mid-winter. Back when the snow was a foot deep and the thermometer didn't get above ten, I wished for this.

But with my hands in hot dishwater and my temperature rising, sweat plopping into the suds below, I was desperately looking for something to salvage this summer evening. I didn't want to be here, but here I was, and I wanted something to make this worthwhile.

It certainly wasn't going to be the smell of the garbage below our back window. We were a day late with the trash pickup because of the Fourth of July holiday. The sun, humidity, and flies made this an odoriferous setting.

The yard was mowed. That was a comfort. I could honestly let it go at least another week before I took my swings around the lot again. But it wasn't enough.

7

Sometimes geese gather in the field behind our house, but today it was barren. The trees were absolutely still.

Then I spied her. Actually I heard her. Soft falsetto sounds came from the direction of the swing set. La la la la. She sang some incomprehensible ode to God.

Her younger brother ran in, slamming the door behind him. "I'll be out in a minute," he yelled out the window with a wild look of determination on his face. "I have to go to the bathroom."

I heard the downstairs door slam. This could take five minutes. This could take an hour. You know how boys are about the bathroom. There are just so many things for a four-year-old to sit and think about.

His older sister was on a swing flanked by another swing and a two-person ride. The sun had baked her little arms a deep brown, and that just made her blue eyes more blue. Her hair, usually a light brown, had turned blond in streaks and was touching her shoulders.

La la la la, she sang, oblivious to me and the neighbors and the birds and the little rabbit running behind her.

She swung back and forth and squinted into the sun. You could see every white tooth in her head, and I thought it was beautiful.

She got off the swing and switched to the two-person ride and rocked back and forth, singing all the while.

She leaned her head back and her hair floated there, suspended above the ground. Then she reached back and touched the limb of a tree, swatting at the leaves. La la la la. She grabbed a leaf and tore it off to look at it. She held it up to the sun and looked through it, squinting again, showing her teeth.

Then she grabbed the limb again and held on, using it to help her swing back and forth, her legs pushing and her arms holding. La la la la.

I heard the toilet flush downstairs. Water running, hands drying. Clomp, clomp and my son was up the stairs and poised at the front door with an excited look.

"Is she still outside?" he asked me with a look of hope.

"Yeah, she's still there."

The front door slammed and he was gone. I heard the sound of an ice-cream truck whose melody I can never get out of my head once I hear it. "Turkey in the Straw" has to be the most annoying and most wonderful sound a truck can make.

She smiled and welcomed him to the swing set, and the picture blurred as I felt water drip into the dishwater again.

La la la la, he took up the strain and the two became one, pushing and pulling, swinging, singing, and playing on that beaten-down, secondhand, green-and-white garage-sale swing set.

And to think I almost missed it.

———◆———

CHAPTER TWO

Sometimes Life Imitates Baseball

Eight months out of the year my wife and I try to take an afternoon walk. It's a walk to "connect," a walk for exercise, and a walk just to be together without seven children clamoring for our attention. Actually, they don't clamor for my attention; they clamor for hers. We take the youngest two in the double stroller and head for our route, which is about two miles.

One fateful day God ordained a confrontation with my deficiencies. There was a very important baseball game on television. My favorite team was playing, tied for the last playoff spot with only four games to go. Every out was important.

In the bottom of the eighth, my wife peeked her perky head around the corner and said, "You want to go for a walk now? I'm ready."

When she says, "I'm ready," I interpret it to mean, "If we

don't go now, pestilence will follow." Actually that's not true. She has little control over pestilence, but if I don't have a really good reason for not going, I feel guilty.

"Sure, let's go," I said.

While she got the kids into the stroller, I put on my big sweatshirt and retrieved my daughter's portable radio and an earphone I can plug into one ear. *Andrea always walks to my right,* I thought. *I'll plug my left ear, and she'll never know the difference. Plus, I only have to turn it on every few minutes, just to make sure my team wins.*

By the time she had the kids ready, I was wired for sound. It was perfect. I had my earphone dangling within my sweater, ready to plug in. I had my lovely wife to my right and a clear sidewalk on which to push the children. All was wonderful on God's green earth.

We passed Mundane and Grace and walked another half block before I turned on the radio.

"The bases are loaded now, with one out here in the bottom of the ninth, and the score remains seven to five."

How in the world would I keep this information from anyone? This was so exciting! But I restrained myself and kept walking.

"It was just such a breakthrough moment for me," came the voice to my right. "I didn't want to do it, but I went ahead and look what happened! It was just so clear."

Usually on our walks I talk about myself, my writing, my job, my frustrations, or what I would like for dinner until we get to the halfway point. But on this walk Andrea had just met with a friend and needed to vent. My chivalry and the game said, "Just let her talk."

I did and listened to two voices at once: "…I was sitting there and I just saw myself…" "…popped up on the left side, it may be playable…" "…she was really in pain and I didn't…" "…makes the catch and there are two down…" "…but I knew I did the right thing!"

"Mmmm," I said.

If she had talked about the weather, who has soccer practice, how much piano lessons cost, or anything on the surface of our lives, I am convinced I would have been able to listen to that final half inning unhindered. But because she had chosen a conversation of depth, I had a queasy feeling in my stomach.

"Strike one…" *I shouldn't be listening to this.* "…And it was because I was vulnerable that she was able to tell me…" "…ball, outside, one and one…" *If she finds out, I'm sunk.* "…And she just opened up and told me her life story…" "…fouled away, one ball, two strikes…" *I'm in big trouble.*

We came to the intersection of Love and Understanding, a busy place always difficult to cross. I made the decision, as painful as it was, to take my earphone out and listen to her, forget the game, forget the last out, forget the bottom of the ninth, just listen to her.

A car waved us through, and as I pushed the stroller, I grabbed the earphone and pulled it out of my ear, but it flopped out and dangled down the front of my shirt like a hissing snake.

"What's the matter?" she said.

I smiled and said, "Nothing," but she knew something was awry. The more she asked, the funnier it seemed to me. I pushed the stroller ever onward, but she stopped and stared.

"I feel really stupid here, like there's something I don't know."

She needed help to move, like a puppy whose leash is caught on a stump.

"I was interested in the ending of this game," I said. I explained the whole sordid affair. Now she looked like a puppy who had been hit with a stump.

"I'm sorry," I said. "I just wanted to hear the last inning, and I shouldn't have."

"No," she said. "I wish you had told me back at the house, and I would have waited until the game was over."

I did not tell her I was afraid of pestilence. We commenced walking again, a little slower now. She did not want to talk. "Go ahead and listen to the rest. You might as well."

I plugged my ear quickly and heard, "Fouled away again, two balls, two strikes, bottom of the ninth, bases loaded, two outs, seven to five, and the playoff hopes hang in the balance."

"All they need is one more out."

"I don't want to hear it."

"Honey, bases loaded, two balls, two strikes…"

"I don't want to hear it," she repeated.

"But it's the bottom of the ninth!"

"I want to walk in peace. Just listen and let me enjoy this beautiful day."

The weather, I thought. *If she had only talked about the weather I wouldn't be in this pickle.*

"Fouled away again, still two balls and two strikes…"

One ear full of sound, one ear silent and hurt. Half my head filled with a picture of green grass, white bases, and the diamond shape of the infield. The other half sensed anger and estrangement. Why does a man have to choose sides of his head? Shouldn't the wife of the author of *The H.I.M. Book*[1] understand that this is a pivotal moment, when past and present converge, when boyhood dreams merge with the rigors of adult life and bring unparalleled joy and satisfaction?

Oh, who am I kidding? I thought. *Just get the last out and let me apologize! I want this game to be over.*

"Fly ball to left field," the announcer said, signaling the end of the game. My heart lightened. This would make it so much easier to say how truly sorry I was. Admitting you're wrong when your team wins and heads to the playoffs is a lot less difficult. I was about to turn off the radio when I heard, "He's under it and makes the ca—HE DROPPED THE BALL! HE DROPPED THE BALL! All three runs score! All three runners score and—oh my, what a heartbreaking loss!"

Awestruck, I stopped and put my head on the stroller. I couldn't move. Couldn't breathe. My wife walked ahead. Oh the agony. *Now we're even,* I thought. *We both feel betrayed.*

Sometimes life imitates art. Other times it imitates baseball.

---

[1] To help you understand a man's mind better, read this in-depth treatise on the Highly Identifiable Male. You'll find lots of laughs and a few unexpected tears as well.

CHAPTER THREE

Tearing Up Mr. Happy

Mr. Happy is on the floor by the trash can, only half a yellow smile visible to the world. Someone has torn him to shreds.

Mr. Happy is one of my son Reagan's paperback books. It describes a place called Happyland, on the other side of the world where the sun shines hotter and the trees are a hundred feet tall.[2]

Mr. Happy has been pieced together more times than I care to admit. Edges are ripped, staples are long gone, pages are marked with pen and pencil, and there are kid stains of cereal and peanut butter and jelly on almost every page.

Until today my wife and I repaired *Mr. Happy* for the sheer joy of watching Reagan walk around with it. Reading *Mr. Happy* is unlike reading any other children's book. It takes a short amount of time and leaves everyone smiling. At the end, Mr. Miserable's life is turned around. What more could you ask?

But Andrea and I have come to a unanimous decision. *Mr. Happy* is beyond human help. *Mr. Happy* is going to that great bookshelf in the sky.

When we broke the news to Reagan, he seemed unaffected. But I know, deep within his heart, there will come a yearning for *Mr. Happy*. One day he will come to me and ask to read it again, and I will have to explain that *Mr. Happy* is no more.

"Do you know why we had to get rid of *Mr. Happy?*" I will say.

"No."

"Because someone tore up your *Mr. Happy*."

"Really?"

"Yes, Son. Life can be that way. People will come along and try to tear up your *Mr. Happy,* but don't you let them."

"I won't, Dad. Do you know who tore up my *Mr. Happy?*"

"Ah, that's the sad part, Son."

And then I will get on my knees, put my arm around him, and get very close to his face before I say these important words.

"Son, *you* tore up your own *Mr. Happy*."

Shock and amazement will fill his face, but these are the conversations a father must initiate.

"Why, Dad? Why would I do such a thing?"

"I don't know why you did it. I don't know if you were angry or tired or sick, but one day we found you walking around with only pieces of *Mr. Happy,* and we had to toss him."

I have met people who enjoy ripping up my joy. I can fight these half-full demons. But I have a harder time fighting Mr. Happy's biggest enemy. He is in the mirror each morning.

---

[2] Roger Hargreaves, *Mr. Happy* (Los Angeles: Price/Stern/Sloan Publishers, 1971, 1980).

———————

CHAPTER FOUR

First Date

O n her desk is a calendar with two very important words scrawled under this Friday. It says "Date Night." Friday night is the evening my world comes to an end.

I've been waiting more than thirteen years for this night. I've been dreading it: her first date. I don't mind telling you it scares me, the woman she is becoming. A friend asked if I liked the fellow taking her out, and I replied, "Not particularly." I wanted him to be the perfect person, the perfect date. I suppose he'll have to do.

It only seems like a couple of hours since Andrea and I brought her home from the hospital, and now it's time for her first date. I can still remember holding her in my arms on the first morning of her life. The anticipation, the mystery of having a child, and then the sudden cry and the soiled diaper awakened me to the truth. Old people, people in their forties, told me it would go by fast, and I believed them. But not this fast.

I have been resigned to this inevitability and have tried to let her go a little each day. A choice here or there, whether to let her wear socks with the sandals or get her hair cut short. Last year she wanted another pierce in the ear and red hair. What will it be next year? But those are little changes. What father in his right mind lets his daughter date at thirteen?

Friday afternoon blew by like a hurricane. She was to be ready at 5:15. There was talk of a quick run to a local department store for last-minute details. A buzz skittered among the siblings who wondered in awe as they saw her with a dress and nice shoes. What's up? Why not the shorts and a T-shirt?

The date arrived in his car at 5:16:44. I know because my watch was the only thing I could really focus on. He rang the doorbell and my daughter met him, smiling. He handed her a single rose and placed a bouquet of flowers in the hands of my wife. They both said, "Thank you," and giggled.

He sat in our living room, my wife and daughter gazing intermittently at the date and the ceiling, wondering where he would take her to eat, what movie they would see. And then it was time to leave. Just like that. All the letting go in the universe cannot prepare you for that moment.

My wife stopped them for one last picture, a little water in her eye, and then the door closed and the two were gone.

The date opened the car door for her. He turned the air conditioning on high because he knew she would appreciate it. He does know her quite well. He took her to a restaurant that served steak because he knew she was apprehensive about eating anything you have to cut with a knife and she wanted a little practice. That's what first dates are for. She had never eaten steak before, and she was nervous about selecting the correct fork to use for the salad. So he showed her. She ate nearly all of the New York strip but allowed him to finish the potato.

Her date drove her to a theater, and they spent forty-five minutes milling about, laughing, talking, waiting for the movie. They ate Reese's Pieces as they watched a romantic comedy. Then he brought her home.

As they stepped into the house, her date opened his arms, much like he had done thirteen years before, and held her tightly for only a moment. She seemed so close, but at the same time so far away.

And before I went to sleep that night in the room next to hers, I gave thanks to the Father above for tiny hands that grow, for Fridays, for the innocence of daughters, and that I hadn't missed the opportunity to be her first date.

CHAPTER FIVE

———◆———

Blowing a Chance on I-65

I was standing by the side of Interstate 65, somewhere in the middle of Indiana, with six screaming children and a hysterical wife, when I realized I would never achieve every parent's dream.

Earlier in the day, all eight of us piled into the car. I turned on the radio to listen, ironically, to Dr. James Dobson's radio program, *Focus on the Family*. It was a tender interview about parenting. I looked in the rearview mirror and counted six beautiful heads.

Then I did what most people do when they listen to *Focus on the Family*. I imagined what it would be like to be interviewed. I gave great, emotional answers and had Dr. Dobson bawling so hard Mike Trout had to go into the other room for a box of tissues.

The program's theme played, and my wife said, "Their story really makes you think, doesn't it?" She hugged the child buckled between us.

"Yeah," I said, thinking about what I would say on program number two the next day. *If they would only try me once,* I thought, *I would hold the record for consecutive days on the program. I have so much wisdom to share. I have so much parental love and understanding flowing through my veins, it's a shame to let it go to waste.*

Traffic was heavy and huge trucks passed on either side, blowing us back and forth between the white lines. We hit Indiana and settled in for a long night. The kids would fall asleep, and I would drive straight on till morning.

As dusk settled, little stomachs took control of the trip. I heard plaintive cries from the back of the car. Like wayward sheep, the children bleated for a fresh pasture of Happy Meals. Unfortunately, I did not have my rod or my staff to comfort them, so I raised my voice in a shepherdly manner and suggested they be quiet.

One of the little sheep, the oldest, kept bleating. Since she is so much like me, her words stung. She has the ability not just to get under my skin, but to get under it, stand up, walk around, do a cartwheel, and kick my eyeballs. To this day no one remembers what pushed me over the edge, but it had something to do with her "tone" and a general disregard of several "severe bleating warnings." (A "bleating warning" is much more serious than a "bleating watch," according to the National Parent Service.)

I can still remember the look in her eyes when, after several threats of "I'm going to pull this car over," I actually did. I was way over on the grass tilting to the starboard side, but you could still feel the trucks pass, as if they were only inches away.

"Get out," I said. They were the only words I needed.

All the air went out of the car. No one breathed, let alone thought of bleating. You could hear a Cheerio drop.

I stomped to the other side of the car and opened the door. The offending sheep was trying to crawl over her siblings toward me, but crawl is not the right word. She was moving like the blob, taking as long as she could to avert the inevitable confrontation.

I grabbed a leg and pulled. The sheep came out of the car in a breach position, crying.

I honestly do not know what I intended to do at that moment. I wasn't going to spank her; she was too big to spank. I wasn't going to leave her there; it would have been unusually cruel to the wolves. I don't even know if I was going to yell at her because before I could open my mouth, my wife burst from the front passenger side, her hair flopping in the wind. With a shriek, she stepped onto the green Indiana grass and yelled, "Don't hurt my baby! Please don't hurt my baby!"

I stopped and looked around, wondering, *Who is this person and what baby is she talking about?* She grabbed my daughter and it was all over. They hugged each other and cried, and I looked out over the cornfield by the highway. The sun was just dipping below the horizon. I turned to our car. All the windows were down, and I saw five mouths agape.

For the next few miles all I could hear was whimpering from the backseat. Sheep sometimes safely graze on such experiences.

And then the dawn broke. I looked at my wife and she wiped her eyes. I thought she was crying, but she was stifling a smile.

"What?" I said.

She paused for effect and then said the words I'll never forget.

"I think we just blew our chance to be on *Focus on the Family*."

CHAPTER SIX

———◆———

Just Trying to Get By

T hree-year-old Kristen was maneuvering behind Megan,
who has long brown hair. It just so happened, as these
things often do, that Kristen's foot firmly, though unintention-
ally, came down on the end of Megan's hair just as Megan
moved forward. Judging from Megan's reaction, this event
caused no small amount of pain, and the noise that did come
forth from that child was like a tornado siren. Yea and verily,
she did wail.

Kristen moved along without much remorse in her sin-
stained heart, though the scream did cause her to jump back-
ward into the wall. I tried to console the injured party with an
explanation, which, in retrospect, wasn't the right thing to offer. When your head hurts, you need someone to lean on, not
to explain things. However, I then said the following sentence,

which I will forever stand behind, and I quote: "She didn't mean it; she was just trying to get by."

That was true. Kristen didn't mean any harm when she caused that clump of hair to come out; she was just trying to move past her sister without provoking her or even making physical contact. She was just trying to get by.

The loud wailing continued as I pondered the principle. There are many people in my life who don't mean to hurt me, who don't intend to make me pay for the pain they're going through, but who nonetheless have the uncanny ability to step right on the end of my hair just as I'm getting up. These are the same people who get in front of me on the expressway at the exact moment I'm in a hurry, or who are overly critical about something I've done when I desperately need a pat on the back. In these and a million other ways, they show they're just trying to get by.

Thanks to my children, I now have a new designation for people in need of a little grace from those around them. They are hereby labeled JTTGB, or "Just Trying To Get By."

You may find them in the grocery line, at the Laundromat, gas station, church, or even in your own home. Watch out for them. Train yourself to spot them. Give grace and mercy to them because, if you're like me, one day it'll be you who's just trying to get by.

CHAPTER SEVEN

Experiencing Dog

I have always hated listening to pet stories, especially when people go on and on about the utter cuteness of their little poochie. (By the way, I refuse to capitalize the name of a dog.)

In my view, the only good pet stories describe: (1) an animal saving a human's life, (2) a pet gnawing off its leg to survive, (3) a pet gnawing off a human's leg to save a person's life, or (4) a pet gnawing off a leg just for fun. Otherwise, don't tell me your pet story.

The worst pet stories are told by those who try to draw a spiritual parallel to life. I recall listening to one contemporary singer draw grand lessons from the life of a new puppy, and the disdain I felt as I thought, *Boy, I'll never do that!*

This was before we purchased pippen, our dog. Pippen (I have to capitalize the first word of a sentence, even if it's a dog's name) came to us highly recommended. The ad said something like, "Good with children, doesn't shed, gnaws at leg, and makes great chapter material in poignant, life-changing books." *That's the dog for me*, I thought, so we brought pippen home at the beginning of a hot summer, and he's been part of the family ever since.

One great spiritual lesson I've learned from the cute little thing (I'm really very sorry about this) is the value of contentment. We have a stake in the backyard and a leash attached to it that will travel in a fifteen-foot radius. It doesn't matter how much food or water pippen has in his dish, how many toys are in his area, or how much sleep the neighbors are trying to get, every time we put him outside, he runs to the end of the leash and paces back and forth, barking and whimpering.

This, of course, wears out the grass in that section of the yard. It also drives those inside the house crazy. "Shut your yap!" we scream affectionately. Hour after hour he paces and pants, straining to the edge of the well-worn path. The only thing that keeps him from the limits of his area is the presence of someone he loves. When one of us ventures into his circle, he jumps, delighted to have company.

I sat down beside him one day and thought deeply about my life. As pippen gnawed on my leg, I looked at my life and my leash. God has given me good things. I have a place to run filled with pleasures, but I'm always straining for more, barking and whining when I don't get something I think I need. I don't fully appreciate the things given me because I'm so focused on what's over there by the swing set or in the neighbor's yard.

But I'm different from pippen in an important way. This makes me sad. He is our dog. Our name and phone number are on his collar. Likewise, I am a child of God. I am a disciple and bear the name of Christ. But as I look closely at my life, my everyday yearnings are not focused on the Master. I don't strain at the end of my leash for him. Much of the time, I'm looking for things that ultimately will not satisfy.

This is the kind of spiritualizing you get in just about any book that includes pet stories, but now I kick into the really deep stuff. Anybody can talk about that leash stuff and the circle of opportunity and blah-blah-blah. Now, I go the extra mile. I'm about to be vulnerable.

You know what I thought as I was sitting there watching my dog gnaw my leg off? *Yeah, but at least I don't drool. And I don't chase my tail. If I had one I might, but I don't.*

That's right, I compared myself to our dog, and sadly, I felt really good about it. He looks for a treat every time he comes in the house and goes to his kennel. That's a big deal to him. How utterly pathetic! I don't do that.

Then I looked at his leg and wondered how it would feel to gnaw it, just a little, but then my kids came home and took him for a walk.

On good days it doesn't feel like I'm on a leash. On bad days you'll find me straining and wearing a groove in the grass as I look in the next yard. My prayer is that I'll recognize all the good things my Owner has given today. I want to be happy just to see him. I want to long for his presence.

When that happens, maybe I'll know what it's like to have a tail.

CHAPTER EIGHT

A Prayer for Every Day

Lord, lift my eyes today from the stuff of earth. Help me see the sun, and if there are clouds, help me see them, too.

Take away my unending desire to know exactly what your will is for my entire life, and give me an unquenchable thirst to know only you today.

When I'm in an argument with friend or foe, deliver me from the need to always be right. Give me instead a desire to love.

Deliver me from the need of things to make me happy.

Except for that new printer.

Okay, deliver me from the printer, too.

When I'm looking for my keys or a parking place today, Lord, I pray you will give me patience instead.

And then I pray you will reward my patience with a really close parking space.

Make me a servant. Deepen my understanding of your love and let my service respond sincerely, not from a sense of duty.

Give me a willingness to at least attempt being content with my circumstances.

Lord, deliver me from the need to keep score.

Show me someone who needs a smile today. Help me give it without reserve.

When someone cuts me off in traffic, give me the grace to remember when I did the same, stupid thing.

Open my eyes to see what you see.

Open my ears to hear what you hear.

Deliver me from the island of *me*.

You who spoke the universe into being, who set the stars in their courses, who formed my DNA, don't just give me a spiritual bypass. Create in me a new heart, a clean heart, a willing heart.

Open my nasal passages and help me smell the newly cut grass and the fresh, clean scent of my little girl's hair.

You who touched the tongue of the dumb, loosen my tongue to speak your praises.

Give me a heart of thanks for fallen leaves, flat tires, wet sneezes, phlegm, and tooth decay, for these things make me long for heaven.

Show me souls today, not just faces.

Show me hurts today, not just anger.

Give tears for dry eyes.

Change the drudgery into work fit for a King's son.

Strip me of pride, sloth, and envy.

Clothe me with humility and vigor, and help me find a good antonym for "envy."

Lord, I look at my child opening a bag of candy. I see the anticipation and expectancy and want this same spirit when I think about you.

Give me a renewed desire for your Word.

If a storm should come, give peace.

If doubt should come, give hope.

If a couple of Jehovah's Witnesses should come, help me not to hide inside the house until they leave. Help me show them a kindness and love they have never experienced.

Most of all, Lord, in every moment of this day, help me see Jesus.

Amen.

CHAPTER NINE

I Climbed Mount Everest, and All I Got Was Frostbite

Into Thin Air by Jon Krakauer tells the story of a 1996 Everest expedition that left four dead and changed the lives of several others. If you haven't read it, I suggest you go to a bookstore and buy another copy of my book, then go to the library and check out *Into Thin Air*. (This is a shrewd new bookselling plan I've devised without the help of Jon Krakauer.)

The stories in this book are heart-wrenching and brutally honest, but the one that captivated me is the story of Beck Weathers. Dr. Weathers, a successful Dallas pathologist, dreamed for years of climbing Mount Everest. Finally, he left his family and set out for Nepal to pursue that dream. When a blinding snowstorm hit the group on top of the mountain, Weathers was left for dead in the snow as the others struggled to survive. No one had the strength to carry him back to camp. If he wasn't dead, his friends thought, he would be soon.

But he was not dead. To the shock of his surviving team-mates, Weathers stumbled upon the group and was given aid. After the ordeal was over, Weathers was left without much of his right arm, all four fingers and the thumb on his left hand were removed, and his nose was amputated and reconstructed with other tissue. In a later interview, Weathers said he saw his facial scars as daily reminders of what's really important.

My wife and kids mean the world to me, and seeing Beck Weathers realize the depth of his feelings for his own family stirred the same feelings in me. I told Andrea his story. "What a wonderful realization," I said with a tear in my eye. "What a great lesson for all to learn. Isn't it astounding how something so poignant and gut-wrenching could come from a book about Mount Everest? It teaches us all a lesson. Wow! Makes me want to climb Everest so I can learn the same thing."

I believed this would help my wife understand a little of the deep feelings underneath my rough exterior. (To be honest, my exterior is more flabby than rough.) Andrea looked at me with her patented quizzical stare. It's a lot like the look a man gets when he's sent to the grocery store for fruit, milk, and diapers and instead brings home a loaf of white bread and a box of Twinkies.

35

"Why," she asked, "did it take nearly freezing to death to get this guy to realize his family mattered? Why did he have to spend tens of thousands of dollars, months away from the ones he loved, and a few fingers to figure out they mean everything to him?"

Shocked and appalled, I called her a metaphor pooper. Earth and sky had converged for me in a wonderful, emotionally charged moment, pouring brilliant sunshine into my soul. I had just experienced a breakthrough, and Andrea called it hollow. I harrumphed about the house, charging her with misdemeanor metaphor assault. But I knew she was right.

Beck Weathers's story moved me because I long to be a better husband and father, but I know I often sacrifice relationships on the altar of my goals. I understand this principle on paper, but in reality it's hard to leave the adrenaline rush of Everest for the duties of home.

Rearing children is a massive proposition. It takes years of hard work and preparation. There is great pain, financial sacrifice, and risk. Rearing children is an Everest assignment. It's more difficult than climbing a real mountain because it is not definable. The beginning and end are blurred, and you have to climb 365 days a year without a break. It's also not glamorous. You look silly driving the kids to band practice in your robe and slippers. But if God has called you to this mountain, it's the only place to be.

I want to climb great pinnacles, stand at the top, and shout to the glory of God. He wants me to walk down one flight of stairs to the toddler nursery.

I want to be interviewed by famous journalists so I can tell the world what a great God I serve. He wants me to be known fully by my children, not through a press release, but as I really am.

I want to give my life and die a martyr in service to the Almighty. He wants me to die to myself a little every day and serve my family.

This is the courageous choice. It is the path of an Everest faith. Truly pleasing God means climbing his mountains, no matter how mundane they may seem, and finishing well. You won't get a medal or a mention in the newspaper, and some may even despise your lifestyle, but the scars you get are worth every step.

CHAPTER TEN

The Girl on the Bike

I was in a cab looking at the back of my boss's head, comparing how much hair we both have and feeling good because he was going to pay for the ride. These are life's little pleasures. A light drizzle misted the windows. Without turning around he asked, "So, what book are you working on right now?"

"Well…," I began. I enjoyed the question way too much. My dreams have been enhanced by this very scenario. More than once I've answered the question and awakened to find myself drooling on the pillow. Now it was no longer a dream; I drank in the moment as the cab paused at a three-way stop. "It's about living as a Christian in the everyday, seeing God's grace in the mundane things, a primer for people whose faith has become…"

The cab pulled into traffic. She came from the left, pedaling quickly toward us. In an instant the bike hit the car, and the rider's face smacked the windshield with a sickening thud.

Blood in her mouth, she slowly pulled herself up, like a wounded animal, groggy and scared. The cab pulled over to the curb.

I got out of the cab and saw a policeman walking toward us. "Hey, a girl on a bike just got hit," I told him. He glanced toward me, and I pointed to the street. She was still in the middle of traffic, leaning against her bike, the chain dangling to the ground. She wobbled a bit as cars passed without stopping or even slowing. I ran to the middle of the street and took her bike.

"I don't know if I'm cut out for this job," she said.

"How long have you been doing it?" I asked.

"Four days."

I helped her to the sidewalk. The policeman had left, and people in the coffee shop were staring out the window at us. The cabdriver immediately suggested she call an ambulance. The girl refused and radioed her company.

"Can you make it back here?" I heard the monotone dispatcher ask. She frowned and rolled her eyes. "I don't think I can ride my bike. I just got hit by a car."

There was blood on her hand now, dripping from the hole in her chin. She started to shake. I grabbed some napkins from inside the coffee shop and brought them to her.

My boss and coworker headed back to work after I assured them I would stay and help with a police report. So it was just me, the rain, the cabby, a young girl crying, and a sea of gawkers. She had short white hair that stuck to her helmetless

39

head. Her ears were full of rings. Her clothes were wet from the rain and looked like they had been purchased from the twenty-five-cent bin at Goodwill. Her corduroy pants hung past the tops of her smooth-bottomed sneakers.

My tie was getting wet, but we stood in the mist as she talked to her dispatcher again. She was not telling the truth about her condition, as if she were afraid of something. We found her a plastic chair by a nearby building, and she sat down and wiped her eyes. The bleeding stopped. I bought her a bottle of water at the coffee shop for $1.37. It's funny how you remember things like that. Maybe I thought I could claim it on my taxes, but last I heard there's still no Samaritan deduction.

"We need to file a report," the cabby said in his thick African accent. He was not unkind, but I could tell the clock was ticking. She sat and cradled the water under her arm, and we stood as the rain washed the pavement.

I felt something for this young girl. In her eyes there was a measurable feeling of lostness, something that made me think she was far from home, far from anyone who cared if she was bleeding on a wet street corner in Chicago. Her eyes were red now, glancing back and forth, waiting for the nonexistent help.

"Let's get in the cab and go file a report," the cabby said again. This time the girl stood and got in the car.

We put her bike, helmet, and courier pack in the trunk and drove three blocks to the police station. She locked her bike at a parking meter, as if she'd done it a thousand times, and walked directly into traffic.

"Hey," I said grabbing her arm, "we're not driving you to the police station so you can walk in front of a bus!"

She smiled—her first expression of innocence. She turned to me and tipped her head back. "Do you think I'm gonna need stitches?"

Her chin was clean now, and I could see a neat hole underneath and the red inside. "Yeah. It's not bad," I lied, "but you'll definitely need stitches."

She swore. She was very good at swearing. It rolled off her tongue like a prayer to the god of streets and sanitation workers. Somewhere, in some distant brick house or apartment or mansion, a mother wondered where her daughter was, and I was beside her, walking into the big-city police station.

She was trembling as the officers on duty told us to either take her to the emergency room or to get an ambulance. She didn't want to call her company again, so I took the radio and sternly told whoever was listening that we were taking her to the hospital.

The last time I saw her, she was in the front seat of the cab, holding the bottle of water.

"What's your name?" I asked.

"Liz," she said.

"Liz, I'm gonna pray for you."

She rubbed her eyes and thanked me, and I walked to the corner and went back to work. For an instant, as they were turning left toward the hospital, I almost ran back and jumped in. Almost. In the moments that followed, I questioned myself.

How far do you go to care for strangers on bicycles who smack into cabs, especially lowly messengers who are almost as unwanted as rats?

I went back to my safe world, grabbed my middle-class computer bag, and headed for the office garage. Emerging in my own car, I found myself inexorably drawn to turn left toward the hospital rather than right toward the expressway. I didn't know whether it was something spiritual or morbid. I encountered lots of construction and broken pavement, packed one-way streets, and no parking. Finally I found half a space, engaged my emergency flashers, and ran into the lobby of the emergency room. The cabdriver spotted me and smiled. He stood and shook hands with me.

"They have taken her into the examination room," he said. "She is going to have stitches."

"Did the police come?" I asked.

"No. They said they are very busy." He pointed to two security guards who stood by the door of the ER. They eyed me suspiciously and rocked on their heels.

"This is my passenger in the cab," the driver said.

The security guards stared, nodded, then looked away. I went to the desk and asked about Liz and her condition. The man behind the counter said she was inside with someone from her company and was having an x-ray.

I gave the cabdriver my name and phone number and told him to call me if he needed a statement. We looked at the scratch on his door and recounted the accident.

"You came to a full stop at the sign," I said reassuringly.

"If I had not stopped," he said, "things would have been much worse."

I nodded.

"Thank you," he said in parting. "This has never happened to me before."

"Me either."

"She told me she had just moved from New York. She lives alone. She has no one."

My car was still where I had parked it, the flashers still going. I don't remember much of the drive home, but I do recall pulling into my driveway, where the faces of the ones I love greeted me.

I pray for Liz, for others who are alone in crowded places, and for eyes to see them.

CHAPTER ELEVEN

The Ninety-Minute Wait

The flu is no respecter of persons, and our family is not immune. The joke in our house is that the kids drink amoxicillin like water. For those who don't know, amoxicillin is generally a pinkish, bubble-gum flavored medicine that cures everything from ear infections to sore throats. It's so good I've lobbied Dairy Queen to add it to their list of Blizzard flavors. Right in front of Butterfinger. No luck yet.

Dinner was on the table one evening when we noticed Ryan getting warm. He was a hunk of burnin' child by the time we called the doctor's office. Then I heard the four words that drastically changed my evening: "Bring him right in." My wife put on her coat. She's usually the one who takes the kids. She nurtures and soothes fevered brows.

Questions arose in my mind like the steam that came off

the stir fry on my plate. Why do women always take this responsibility? Why don't men initiate more often? Why was she
the one who called the doctor? Do I want to give up a hot meal?

"Would you like me to take him?" I heard myself ask.

Andrea draped Ryan around my neck as though he were
my Olympic gold medal. I made my way with him to the winner's podium, the doctor's office waiting room.

There, my puffy-cheeked and red-faced son quietly sat in a
chair beside me, and we began our longest night together. It
might not have been so long if we hadn't had such boisterous
company.

Two mothers and three children waited ahead of us. They
had been there awhile. The mothers appeared to be veterans. I
could tell by their dazed looks. One of the moms said little during the ordeal. However, I distinctly recall two of her sentences:
"I'm going to smack you if you don't sit down," she said at one
point, and, "You can just forget about that television program
you wanted to watch!"

The other mom intently read a magazine article while her
son, Jimmy, bounced off the walls. Of course I've changed
Jimmy's name to protect him (and me).

Every five minutes Jimmy's mom said, without taking her
face from the pages of the magazine, "Jimmy, settle down. I
told you to settle down. This is the last time I'm going to tell
you. Settle down. Jimmy, did you hear me?"

We had been there a half-hour, and Jimmy had not settled
down. Once he bounced off the walls particularly hard and

banged into another child. That time his mother actually put the magazine down, stood, and said, "Jimmy, settle down. This is the last time I'm going to tell you."

This really impressed Jimmy. He opened his mouth and said, "Okay," then proceeded to bounce off more walls. His mother pulled her magazine back into its locked and upright position and continued reading.

Nearly two hours later we were in the examining room. Ryan's fever had abated and he anxiously awaited Dr. Akl.

"Who is the biggest troublemaker here?" Dr. Akl said in his Middle Eastern accent. He calls all our kids his troublemakers and it makes them smile.

I wanted to tell him the biggest troublemaker was Jimmy, but Dr. Akl probably already knew that.

He looked, massaged, listened, tapped, probed, and then diagnosed the problem. He showed me the infected tonsils. He told me the difference between acetaminophen and Motrin. He calmed my fears, reduced the fever further, and pre-scribed—you guessed it—amoxicillin.

Most days I don't need a good doctor. Most days I drive by his office and never think about it. And most days I don't give thanks for a truly amazing servant and his gentle ways. Until I needed that doctor, I had never realized I could wait ninety minutes for anyone and walk away utterly happy.

—◆—

CHAPTER TWELVE

Treetop!

I love being the last person my child sees before he closes his eyes at night. Bedtime is warmth and closeness, a night-light, and a favorite book. Or it can be hell on earth, take your pick.

A beloved exercise I enjoy is analyzing the things I say and sing to my children at this crucial time. It's scary when you closely examine what we put in their little minds just before the lights go out.

Reagan used to holler one word before I turned out the light. "Teetop!" he would yell, meaning "treetop." After singing "Rock-a-Bye, Baby" to him a few hundred times, I started thinking about the meaning of the shocking words.

Rock-a-Bye Baby is in the treetop. Already I see years of counseling and a possible foster family. Who in their right mind places baby and cradle in the treetop?

What happens when the wind blows? The cradle rocks. Pretty soon the wind is howling up there, like a scene from a bad tornado movie, and the bough breaks. It doesn't take Isaac Newton to figure out what's going to happen next. The cradle and Rock-a-Bye Baby plummet to the ground. When we sing, "cradle and all," we tickle our infant and giggle, then wonder why we have such a violent society!

Another favorite of my children is "Hush, Little Baby."

Little Baby is in the process of being enabled by Papa. It's clear that Little Baby is caught up in materialistic tendencies. And why not? Look at what Papa says:

"Hush, Little Baby, don't say a word. Papa's gonna buy you a mockingbird." Buying affection is one thing, buying silence is dysfunctional.

I don't know about you, but if I'm Little Baby, I'm going to hold out for more than a mockingbird. Then, and I'm sure The Society for the Prevention of Cruelty to Animals has something to say about this, Papa promises to purchase a diamond ring if the mockingbird won't sing. But he doesn't say how long they are going to wait. Is it a year? A month? A couple of hours? Maybe the bird is a slow learner.

Now the materialism really kicks in, because Papa is already anticipating that diamond ring turning to brass—or maybe it's cubic zirconium. If there's a defect, Papa's gonna save the receipt and exchange that thing for a looking glass. Excuse me, but don't let this guy take care of the company Christmas present next year.

Papa anticipates the mirror getting "broke," which is poor English, and says he will give the child a billy goat. This is where the song really breaks down. I can see excitement over a dog named "rover," but what on earth is a little kid supposed to do with a billy goat, a cart and a bull, or a horse and cart? Is this child destined to be a nineteenth-century farmer?

The mockingbird and the dog are unable to utter a sound. My guess is the animals have been so traumatized they can't see straight, let alone bark or sing. And why would they? They were bought in hopes of getting Little Baby to hush! If you ask me, these animals are lucky to get out of there alive. These are probably the same parents who put Rock-a-Bye Baby in the treetop!

I think about this, sitting on my children's beds at night, waiting for them to become calm. I don't want to let any of this get by without close scrutiny.

Then I hear someone in the next room reciting the children's poem about mother monkey. Listen to the horror:

Three little monkeys jumping on the bed. One fell off and bumped his head.

Mama dials 9-1-1.

"Monkey emergency, how may I help you?"

"Yes, my little monkey just fell off the bed and bumped his head."

"Is he sitting up? Is he crying?"

"Yes, he's sitting up. He's not crying though, he's just watching the others jump on the bed."

"I'll get a doctor on the line, but you'd better tell the other ones to stop jumping on the bed. Okay?"

"Okay."

Mama monkey wags a finger in their general direction. "No more monkeys jumping on the bed," she says. "Okay, I'm going to count to five, and if you monkeys don't stop..." The monkeys disregard her. They've heard this before. The doctor picks up the phone.

"Keep him as quiet as you can and give him some liquid Tylenol, the banana flavor. But they must stop jumping this instant!"

"I'll try, Doctor. I'll try." But Mama monkey fails. Soon the doctor is back on the phone asking if she's ever heard of the book *Tough Love*.

I shouldn't be so hard on Mama monkey. She's just a single parent doing the best she can. Dad is either absent or gone altogether.

I now sing kinder, gentler versions of these bedtime songs. Learning from modern psychology, I've taken Rock-a-Bye Baby out of her tree and given her a safe place. "Hush, Little Baby" has now become, "Go Ahead Little Baby, Express Yourself." And the little monkeys have a much more stable home life. They now have an intact family with liberal usage of time-outs, and both parental figures share in the monkey-rearing responsibilities.

It pays to think through these issues while your children are young. If you decide to stay with the original versions of these ditties, I pity you. Especially if you don't save the receipt for the mockingbird.

CHAPTER THIRTEEN

Flashing Clocks

The clocks are flashing 12:00 at my parents' house tonight. I know this even though I am five hundred miles away. When you get a little older, things like setting the time on a VCR or microwave aren't a priority. If the machine works, who cares what time it is? When you're older, you're just thankful you can still see the numbers.

As you move toward the evening of life, little things like this don't bother you. You don't worry as much about the ironing or even bugs in your salad. I've watched my parents shoo insects big enough to perform in a circus act from their dinner plates and then go ahead and finish the meal.

"He won't eat much," my father says, smiling.

My parents' home is a peculiar mix of modern technology and antiques. I think they're the only couple in America with caller-ID on a big black rotary phone, the kind that weighs as much as the space shuttle.

Look in the refrigerator and you'll find a few old things as well, things that should have been disposed of in the Hoover administration. Things that are growing. My parents lived through the Depression, so it's no surprise they want to save small bits of food rather than toss them out. Who knows what they're going to do with that last piece of salami they couldn't finish after Nixon's resignation? I have confidence they'll think of something. If not, they'll just buy another refrigerator. I think they're up to seven in the basement.

I have to weigh my desire to call or write my folks. If I write (which I never do), I am able to communicate coherently my love for them. However, I don't get to find out who died last week.

"Hi, honey, they're having Harlow Skruggin's funeral today. You remember him."

"No, I'm afraid I don't."

"Oh sure you remember. He married Jenny Krachbarrel over on Weasel Creek. You went to school with their son, Buford."

"No, I don't think I did."

"Aw, don't be silly. We went over to Harlow's house to help get the pig out of the tree, and you boys got too close to the sludge pond by their gas well, and — oh, you were probably too young to remember that."

"Yeah, I don't think that was me, but what happened at the sludge pond? I'm dying to know."

"No, it couldn't have been you because you weren't born yet."

These are humble people who don't have all the answers. They'll admit they can't remember the questions half the time. But they're willing to listen when you need it. You can tell who they are the moment you meet them. Just talking with them feels like home.

I wish there were more people like them around today, and not just because we need a place to store a side of beef. No, we also need free baby-sitting. Plus our children need role models who will admit their foibles.

Not long ago my mother was walking through the mall and decided to break down and buy a CD she'd been wanting. There's no question she had enough money to get it, but when you're older, you measure your purchases. You weigh important factors, like *How many times will I be able to listen to this before I forget where I put it?*

Shortly afterward, when I dropped by to shovel out her refrigerator, she told me about her purchase.

"I knew right where the music store was," she said. "I've been around that mall a hundred times. I walked in the store and went toward the back to the classical section. As I passed the cashier's desk, a young girl asked if she could help me. I said, 'No, I'm here to pick out a CD.' She looked at me funny, but I just kept going. So many people assume that if you're old you don't know where you're going, so I just put my head down and walked to the back.

"I was all the way to the last aisle before I realized I was in a shoe store," she laughed.

When she passed the girl at the front desk, my mother waved and smiled without a word. No doubt the other employees heard about this crazy old bird who was looking for CDs amid the Buster Browns. I'm sure they had no idea that a great woman had just walked through their midst.

CHAPTER FOURTEEN

Panthers and Cheetahs

Three of our children like to play Panthers and Cheetahs, a game that puts them on their hands and knees. The object of the game is to growl and roam the house until one decides the game is over. The wild animals prance up and down stairs, into the family room, laundry room, and kitchen. Shannon is seven, Ryan is six, and Kristen, who calls herself the baby, is two.

Suddenly there is a great commotion and Ryan runs into the room. He puts his head on the couch and weeps bitterly. It is not the cry one gives when a limb is detached, but it is close.

"What's the matter?" Father cheetah asks.

"Shannon said...I couldn't...be a cheetah anymore."

I do not understand the minds of cheetah cubs, so I decide to enter into this strange world. "Why not?" I ask.

There is no response. The cheetah sobs continue.

"Shannon, come up here," Father cheetah beckons.

Mother cheetah looks at Father cheetah as if to indicate he should stay in his den and not get entangled in this power play. But Father cheetah will not be deterred.

A few seconds later Shannon submissively crawls into the room. She is not growling. There is a slight smirk on her face as she looks at the pain of Brother cheetah.

"Shannon, why can't he be a cheetah?" Father cheetah asks in all seriousness.

She pauses to think and finally explains, "Because panthers don't like cheetahs."

Father cheetah turns to Mother cheetah and mutters, "Racist."

"I thought you were a cheetah," he says.

"No, I'm a panther. He's a cheetah and the baby is a cheetah."

The baby appears at the top of the stairs, growls, then retreats to safety under the kitchen table. A few minutes later the panther relents and Brother cheetah crawls back downstairs to join the pack.

All is quiet for about three minutes, when Brother cheetah again ascends, weeping uncontrollably. The pain seems even worse than the first time.

"What's wrong now?" Father cheetah asks in even tones.

The cheetah is trying hard to explain, but all he can do is snort. "*Snort, snort, snort*...Shannon told me...*snort, snort*...I mean the panther told me...*snort, snort*...I can be a chee-tah...*snort, snort*...but I can't hunt for food!"

This is a world that will pass away all too quickly. Soon I fear the innocence of panthers and cheetahs will be lost.

A few days later I am talking to Shannon one-on-one, and I can see the innocence fade before my eyes and ears.

"I wish I could be a mommy," she says.

"And not a panther?"

She smiles.

"Why do you want to be a mommy?" My heart aches at the thought of her grown and with a family of her own.

She thinks.

"Is it because you like children?"

"Yeah."

"How many children would you have?"

"Five."

"Do you think you would work or stay home with the kids?"

"I'd work."

"Okay. And what would your husband do?"

She looks at me like I have three heads.

"What husband?"

Ahh, I think, *there's still time. Still time.*

———

CHAPTER FIFTEEN

Ripped Seams and Baby's Screams

Women talk about the agony of childbirth, but the waiting really takes a lot out of the father. We have delivered (and I say "we" because I have been present at each of our seven children's births) at three different hospitals. Three because I am poor at following directions and even poorer at asking for them. Every nerve ending in my body signals panic when it comes time to get there.

Some expectant fathers must learn to contend with expectant mothers who rush to the delivery room at every twitch. I have the opposite trouble. The baby's head could be showing and my wife will say, "Let's wait a few more minutes. We don't want to get there too early."

The Saturday our fifth child was born, my wife awakened me to say, "The kids are watching *Little Mermaid*. I'm going out."

This could only mean one thing. Garage sale. I knew as soon as she said those words that she was going to have the baby that day. Nothing excites and relaxes my wife like a good garage sale, especially one sponsored by an entire subdivision. Big things were ahead.

Thirty minutes later I was standing, holding a bowl of cereal, when Andrea sauntered through the front door. It was damp outside, but her sweatpants seemed a bit more wet than they should be.

"My water broke near Kmart," she said without emotion. She knows it's better to give me a landmark than the actual road name.

"What?!?" I screamed, raisin bran spilling on the counter. Fortunately, it was generic raisin bran and not the expensive stuff. "Why did you come back to the house? You should have called from the hospital!"

"Nonsense," she said, putting down a fifty-pound bag of clothes. "I only stopped once more after it broke. I think I'll take a walk around the neighborhood."

After an hour I convinced her to call the hospital, and when I got on the line they urged me to drag her in. The kids were excited as we drove away, knowing we would soon return with a little brother or sister.

My heart raced. Adrenaline pumped through my driving foot. All my paternal instincts kicked in because I knew this was my only legitimate chance to break the speed limit. But the gas gauge was on red.

59

"Sorry about that," she said. "I forgot to tell you it needs gas."

I screeched into the filling station, sloshed five dollars' worth of unleaded somewhere near the tank, threw money at the attendant, then careened toward the hospital. Even with the fifth baby I was nervous, mostly because my wife was treating the whole event like she was having a mole removed.

When we arrived the nurses calmed me and handed me some clothes in a bag marked "Large." I took the bag to a tiny bathroom and opened the bag. I was skeptical. I put my feet in and slowly pulled up the pants. The slower I went, the better chance I thought I'd have.

For a moment I forgot baby number five and was whisked back to a particular year of grade school. I'd had a growth spurt (much like the growth spurts I have every year). When picture time rolled around, I tried on the only suit to my name. The sleeves came halfway up my arms, and the buttons were a good four inches away from the button holes. I was in deep trouble.

It was déjà vu with the hospital garb. When the pants finally reached my waist, they were so tight I looked like a shrink-wrapped walrus. I moved like Frankenstein.

I figured the shirt might cover a multitude of groaning seams, so I pulled it as far down as I could. I stepped sideways and opened the bathroom door. My wife looked at me, grabbed her stomach, and said, "I told you not to make me laugh. It hurts too much."

About that time I noticed a funny feeling on my right side. I wedged my shirt up and saw father flesh protruding from the pants. I discovered later I was the first in the history of the hospital to experience a "gown blowout." The nurse came in and covered her mouth with her hand.

"I think you underestimated me," I said.

"I'll get you another one," she replied. Andrea continued to giggle and ask that I stay out of sight. In a few minutes the nurse returned.

"Here's a large for you."

"THIS IS A LARGE!" I said, humiliated.

Friends howl when I tell that story and others we've collected. Though the details differ with each birth, the outcome has always been the same: I have felt a sense of unforgettable awe and wonder.

At some point Andrea will look at me with Bambi eyes. (Don't write and tell me Bambi is a boy, I know.) At some point I will desire to pounce on her and do a reverse Heimlich maneuver, but I'll realize I can't. Birthing is a process. You wait nine months; you wait a few hours more.

With Kristen, the doctor came in every few minutes to shake his head and say, "Baby don't wanna come out. Don't understand it."

I wondered how long he went to school to learn that brilliant bit of medicine. I held my tongue. I knew he had more knowledge than me. At least that's what I hoped.

At 10:30 P.M. that Saturday, my wife was squealing and the contractions were frequent. In only twenty minutes she had come further than in the past twelve hours. It was time to start

61

pushing. Suddenly I saw a sight that filled me with wonder. There in the doctor's hands was the head of my fifth child. And then the shoulders, arms, and—whoop—there she is, the whole umbilicaled baby, wet and pink and crying.

"You have a little girl," the doctor muffled through his mask. *What a wonderful man,* I thought. *What a fine, educated, wise medical professional.* The nurse cleaned and warmed Kristen, then put her on the chest of the wide-eyed woman who is my wife. The thing that made her belly so big only moments before now looked her directly in the eye. Andrea cried and said hello to Kristen Rebecca. I tried to focus the camera but couldn't.

I will never know the closeness my wife felt at that moment, never understand what it's like to nourish a child from her flesh. This is why it's so hard being a father. You get to burst clothing and speak words of encouragement, but as much of a participant as they say you are, you still feel like an outsider. A woman endures the pain of childbirth. A man endures the alienation of the same.

Like life, giving birth is filled with a few spectacular moments and a lot of mundane ones. You drive fast and watch a miracle, but in between there's a lot of standing around. Then it's over and you're left with a life to mold and a two-year fight with the insurance company.

CHAPTER SIXTEEN

———

Enough?

I suppose we all want our lives to count, to amount to something in the end. In the beginning we please our parents, then our teachers, then our spouse. Then at some point we realize we were really just trying to please ourselves all along, and we've made a mess of the whole thing. There must be more.

I am contemplating these things while my children lament their marinated chicken. The questions before me are "What is the meaning of my existence?" and "How much do we have to eat before we get dessert?" Life screams at me during these moments, the ordinary everyday happenings, such as when my four-year-old puts on the leopard mask and terrorizes her younger brother.

Other men my age are winning Pulitzer Prizes. I saw a college buddy on a news broadcast just the other night. He was standing by the Washington Monument, understanding big issues and conveying them to the anchors in New York or

Atlanta. I secretly wondered how much these guys have to eat to get dessert.

Much of our lives is measured by who we want to be or who we used to be. We spend very little time content with who we are.

I used to host a national radio program. The job was fulfilling. When I stopped hosting it, I looked at a handful of letters that represented a dozen years. *Is this all there is?* I wondered. *What would I have received at the end of twenty years? Would it matter? Should it?*

Can it be enough to sit and read to my children at night, tell them to be quiet, read some more, threaten them with bodily harm, finish the chapter, and tuck them into bed? Is it enough to experience life with a woman who loves me and children who don't like chicken?

I admit I am losing my desire to be great. I read exotic books about adventurers who have achieved the impossible, correspondents who have lived dangerously, and men and women who have done great things but left scattered souls of loved ones in the wake of their success.

Outside my window walk four people carrying coats and lawn chairs. They head toward a baseball field behind our house. Two couples—one old, one middle-aged. They are going to see their son or grandson muff a few ground balls and strike out. Cars pass along the street nearby; people hurry to appointments and important tasks. There is nothing the world would call great about watching a few gangly kids play baseball on a Saturday morning, but this family's choice to go see a child's game may be the most heroic thing I witness all day.

The pull of success and the desire for more call my wayward heart. It is a siren that says what I have is not enough. Motivators tell me to reach for the stars. Successful people say risk is the key to the good life.

But I have my stars around the kitchen table. I am at great risk of losing this moment; I can squander what God has given me by grasping for something I'll never really enjoy in the end, or I can choose the more heroic path that celebrates this day, this chicken.

I hear a still small voice whispering now above the din of the table: "Let me make you great," it says. "Two more bites and you get dessert."

---

CHAPTER SEVENTEEN

100 Percent Life

Some people believe that a person who craves potato chips is really angry at his mother. Others look for hidden meanings behind your choice of salad dressing, I suppose. I've decided there is just too much analysis, and I made that discovery on a green rug at my son's preschool.

Two days a week he sits cross-legged on the floor, pretzel style, with pictures of trees and geese on the walls behind him. The learning center is tucked away in the woods by a small fishing lake, and each time I take him I'm reminded of my childhood.

I normally assign my wife the duty of teacher's aide. It's a woman's thing, you know. But this time Andrea's pregnancy and my lack of a good excuse landed me among the spry and bouncy.

Miss Jenny and Miss Jackie smiled and welcomed me to the theme of the day: wind. I brought the Cheez-Its (low sodium) and two types of juice. Only 100 percent will do for Miss Jenny and Miss Jackie. I had no idea how many juices there are on the market, so I had some difficulty choosing.

The day began by Miss Jenny calling us together and saying, "Maybe we'll have Mr. Chris try to guess the names of all the children at the end of class."

It was my first panic attack of the week. I tried to remember mnemonic devices, matching faces with mental nametags. But what good is a mnemonic device if you can't remember it?

I could remember my son's name, that was one. Jordan had red sweatpants. That was easy. Red-Jordan. Keith had a new haircut, and Matthew was back from California. Okay, Keith-cut and MatthewCal. Kelly's voice sounded like Sally on Charlie Brown, cute and precise. Kelly Brown.

Then I looked at the other names. Murtuza, Graciella, Gabriella, Marina, Vince, Jennifer, Austin. I felt helpless.

The roll was called, and each child talked about something important in his or her life. We heard a story about wind and created wind by flapping a parachute.

The letter for the day was "R." We used our magic index finger to trace the big "R" and the little "r" in the air.

My son stood, took my hand, and led me to the snack table while everyone else worked on their kites, paper bags with strings tied in a loop.

Then we went back to the green room. He sat in my lap while I looked at all the different faces and considered the various backgrounds all the children had come from.

I spent the whole time thinking about what would come of this excursion. Surely there was some great lesson in this ordinary day at the preschool. What could I write? Would I remember all the names? What was the fascinating thing that eluded my powers of observation?

Then it hit me, there on the bright green carpet, with Jordan blowing little yellow Ping-Pong balls across the table and Vince asking for seconds on grape juice. Perhaps the flash of understanding happened as I looked at Marina's bright pink sweater or saw Murtuza's smile.

Whatever it was, I saw clearly that sometimes you need to do life without analyzing it. Sometimes you ought to put away your pen and pad and just sit. Enjoy the view.

Of course there are times for reflection. There are times to put our lives under microscopes and figure out the minutiae. But there are also times just to sit back and let it happen.

And that's what I did the rest of the day. I enjoyed the laughter and games, the stories, the wind, and the "r" review. I enjoyed the walk outside and the squirrels, the wind against my face, and the reflection of the trees in the water.

I didn't need analysis, just 100 percent Life.

CHAPTER EIGHTEEN

Simple Pleasures

All around you at the corner of Mundane and Grace are double-take gifts, things you must look at twice before you see their real value.

Squirrels that stop and look at you.

Acorns on the ground.

A smile.

Just the right amount of change for the toll booth.

Listening to wedding vows.

An in-tune guitar.

Geese in flight.

A flapping flag of red, white, and blue.

Seeing a veteran's salute.

Individually wrapped slices of cheese.

A new toothbrush.

A cool drink on a hot day.

Working hard and feeling the sweat.

A fresh can of tennis balls.

Finding the television remote after months of looking.

Tree limbs low enough to climb.

A good flat rock to skip across the surface of the water.

Catching your spouse unaware with a kiss.

The feel of water on your hands.

Antibacterial soap.

A crisp apple.

The wagging of a dog's tail.

Being at the end of a long line and hearing, "I'll take you
down here."

Catching the mosquito on the first swat.

A full tank of gas.

A crystal-clear window.

Antacid tablets.

Hearing the words, "I forgive you."

Finding pictures you forgot you had.

The first snowfall.

A light that stays green just a little longer.

A phone call from someone you were just thinking about
calling.

Play-Doh.

The smell of a leather baseball glove.

Walking onto an empty playground and feeling like a king.

A milkshake.

Watch bands that last.

An empty dishwasher.

Holding hands.

Visiting Andy and Barney in Mayberry.

Thanksgiving dinner.

Leftovers the day after Thanksgiving.

Taking out the trash a week later and finally getting rid of those bones.

Taking the risk to say, "I love you."

Hearing, "Dad, can you help me with this?"

Marbles.

Being in church with your whole family.

Tickling your kids until they beg you to stop.

Tickling some more.

Pumpkin pie.

Taking a walk for no reason.

A dozen roses.

A check that really is in the mail.

A bright star.

The smell of pine.

Presents.

Red sweaters.

Eggnog.

Sandals.

Footprints in the sand.

A foal of a donkey.

Tears in a garden.

A crown of thorns.

An empty tomb.

———◆———

CHAPTER NINETEEN

Her Hair Was Like Goat Cheese (or Something Like That)

A few months ago I called my wife from work to talk about some really important things. Are we under nuclear attack? Should I pick up a gallon of milk? After considering these, Andrea informed me she had a sitter for a couple of hours, and she asked, "Do you want to meet me for lunch?"

Does my HMO delay paying my medical bills? Do my pants need ironing? The thought hadn't crossed my mind, but the prospect made my heart leap. Good food and great company in a neutral setting? Yes!

"Where do you want to meet?" I asked. She suggested the fish place I like because I can be filled with brain-enriching fish and she can get her favorite salad for only $3.99. This is another reason I wanted to go out: She doesn't order filet mignon or steak marinated in myrrh; she eats little green things that grow on the ends of plants and don't cost much.

I told her I would be at the restaurant at about 11:45.

"Oh," she said in that special tone wives use when they're unpleasantly surprised but don't want to show it. I figured she wanted to continue shopping or doing errands until noon so I said, in that little hurt tone husbands who like to pout rather than express themselves use, "You don't have to get there until 12:00. I'll just try to make it by 11:45."

"Okay," she said happily.

I drove the Eisenhower Expressway anticipating all the things we'd discuss. I was expectant. No children. No worrying about messy tables. Unless I get into an angry halibut-tossing mood, of course. Just us, just like when we were dating.

Dating me was an extremely low-budget affair. I'm embarrassed to tell you how low-budget I was. A "meal out" consisted of walking to the grocery store for a jar of pickles and eating them on the way back. So when I arrived at 11:47, I was excited to sit and wait for my lovely wife and think of how far we'd come.

The hostess led me to a table we'd frequented before. *How fitting,* I thought. I looked at the menu and ordered water (of

73

course) and said I was waiting for my wife. Every twenty seconds I looked up to catch that first glimpse. I wanted to see her first and tell her how it made me feel.

At noon I began to get concerned. Where could she be? 12:05 came and went. Where is she? I had been expecting this meal. I had built myself up for it, and now our baby-sitting hours were running out. Didn't she value the relationship? Was shopping so important that it came before spending time with her beloved?

Then, because I'm a guilt-ridden American male who doesn't listen as closely as he ought, I thought, *Did she say the fish place on Butterfield Road or the fish place on 75th Street?*

Uh-oh.

Big time uh-oh.

Uh-oh squared.

My heart sank to my lower intestine and rushed up to my pituitary gland and then ran down and knocked on my liver, but nobody was home. Was my wife waiting for me in another restaurant? I looked for a telephone, but I had no change. Then I thought, *How much do you tip for a glass of water?*

The waitress walked by and I felt I had to order a bowl of soup or something, so I did. Then I felt guilty about it. She left and I rose to get some change from my car. I passed a few booths along the wall right behind me. There in the first booth was a striking young lady with her head down, reading a magazine.

At first I looked away because I did not want to be tempted by her beauty. But the outfit she was wearing looked familiar. I did a double take. Her hair was like a thousand goats running down a hill. (Hey, it worked for Solomon.) Her nose was like a tower—not a big tower, just a medium-sized tower with two entrances.

Bless my soul, it was my wife!

"Hey," I said.

"Oh hi. Did you just get here?"

"No," I said. "I've been here twenty minutes right over there. Two tables away."

Twenty minutes lost. Twenty minutes of conversation we'll never get back. I fought back feelings of blame. I wanted to be angry. Then I looked into her eyes. One of the thousand goats was caught in her eyelash. I brushed it away, and I smiled. She sneezed and I offered her a hanky so she could blow her tower. She thanked me.

We had a wonderful time. We talked and she read some thoughts from her magazine, which she wouldn't have been able to read if we'd made contact when I first arrived.

I realized then that sometimes the thing we're looking for in life—the thing we're yearning for, the thing that will bring us true happiness and joy and peace—isn't over by the door with the bright lights and commotion. It's not at another place down the road.

Nope.

Sometimes the thing we're looking for is just out of sight, only two tables away.

CHAPTER TWENTY

Uncle Pooch

Inside my guitar is a rattlesnake rattle. When I play for kids, I take it out and shake it and tell them wild stories about how I came by this reptilian relic. But the truth is, my Uncle Pooch gave it to me.

He showed his love by giving me my first real guitar and telling lots of great stories. Pooch said the rattle would make my guitar sound better; it would make the wood and string vibrations "resonate." It sounded plausible at the time.

Pooch, whose real name is my middle name, Howard, never married. He took care of his mother until she died and then helped give his brother a second chance at life. I remember the feel of his chinaberry tree next to the pump house, the bass boat, and the smell of sawdust in his shed.

After Uncle Pooch had his teeth pulled, he decided dentures were just too much work, so he didn't use them. The only time I saw him dressed nicely was the day I saw him in his casket. At his funeral people stood around the room talking, weeping, laughing, repeating his stories. That's the way he was, in the background, bringing people together.

In his kitchen, amid the sizzling aroma of fried trout and the smoke of Camel cigarettes, I would sit and listen. His stories were set in the woods, where he felt most comfortable, or on a lake in Maryland.

Uncle Pooch did not finish school, because his father decided Pooch had had enough learning. There was plenty of work to keep the boy busy. The only discretionary time he had was at night, and this presented some of my uncle's best story material.

One night, when Pooch was still a young boy, he decided to go possum hunting. The hides of possums meant cash in those days, and they were about the easiest game to catch. Pooch had no gun, just a flashlight and a burlap sack. The procedure was simple: Find a possum, scare him so he lies still, and put him in the sack. Repeat until daylight.

Everyone knows hunting is best when you do it with someone else, especially someone who has a dog, so Pooch went to the house of Fred McCallister, many years his senior, and woke him up. Pooch was known to pester Fred into hunting, much to the chagrin of Fred's wife, Ethel. (I am not making up these names.) Fred agreed, and off they wandered into the hills, less than a mile from where I grew up. I was always excited that he was talking about a place I knew, even though it wasn't wilderness anymore. Back in Uncle Pooch's day there were only a few scattered homes along the dirt path they called a road.

Uncle Pooch and Fred had been at it for a couple of hours with no luck when finally, at the bottom of a gully, Fred's dog treed something. They shone the light into the branches and saw two big eyes looking back at them from a dizzying height. They couldn't get a clear look, but the animal was definitely something out of the ordinary.

"It's not a coon," Pooch said.

"Nope," Fred said. "Too big to be a squirrel."

"How are we gonna get it down outta there? We can't climb up and get it—the thing'll eat us up."

Fred moved around the tree once more and shone the light from head to tail.

"Here's what I want you to do. Go up the hill to Tooten Edwards's house." Tooten's real name was Clarence, but when you have a nickname like Tooten, you use it. "Ask him if we can borrow his gun. I think we've treed a mink."

Pooch knew the kind of money a mink pelt would bring. The more they looked, the more they decided their ship had just come in. This was definitely a mink. So he climbed the hill as Fred kept the flashlight steady on the mink. This part of the story would always become more involved, with Pooch falling into the creek and running into trees and brier patches. By the time he made it to Tooten's house, it was in the wee hours of the morning.

He knocked on the door and waited. He heard scuffling inside, and soon Tooten opened the door in his long johns, his hair sticking up in the back.

"Howard, do you know what time it is?"

"I'm sorry to get you out of bed, Mr. Edwards, but Fred McCallister and I were out hunting and…we were wondering…"

"What is it?"

"Well, we've treed a mink down in that big oak at the bottom of the hill, and we can't get it out of there. We were wondering if you'd let us use your gun?"

Tooten scratched his head and retreated into the darkened house. A few minutes later he came back on the front porch with his .22 rifle. To Pooch's surprise, he was fully dressed.

"Mind if I go with you?" Tooten said. "I've never seen a mink before."

The two made their way down the hill in the pitch black and eventually reached the tree. Inevitably, at this point Uncle Pooch's audience expected Fred to be asleep and the mink to be long gone, but not so.

"He's still there," Fred said, shining the light for Tooten to see.

Tooten squinted and took a long look into the tree. "So that's what a mink looks like. Well I'll be."

They stood as hill people will do, silently sizing up the situation. They hadn't thought far enough ahead to the hardest decision of the evening: Who would actually shoot the mink?

"It's your gun," Pooch said. "You ought to shoot it."

"Yeah, but you boys found it," he protested. "If I don't hit him right, it'll ruin the hide."

It was decided that Pooch and Fred would reap the financial rewards, but because it was his gun, Tooten would shoot it. He stood back a few feet and supported himself on a stump, pushed his John Deere cap a little higher, and took dead aim.

At the crack of the gun the animal went limp and crashed through the branches. It fell with a thump into the dead leaves at Pooch's and Fred's feet. They directed the flashlight for a closer look. Tooten rushed to their side and knelt to see the accuracy of his shot. (At this point in the story Pooch would pause and imitate the shock on Tooten's face.) After a long while Tooten stood and glared at my uncle and his friend. This was no mink.

"Howard," Tooten said sternly, "you got me out of bed at three o'clock in the morning and dragged me down here so I could shoot my own cat!"

At that, everyone in the room would howl, even if they'd heard the story twenty-five times. It was almost better having heard it before, knowing what was going to happen, watching it unfold again and again.

Stories are like that. They vibrate in your head and resonate in your life. They help you connect the past with today and give meaning to seemingly meaningless events. They make an ordinary hunting trip a lasting memory.

I've yet to locate a guitar specialist who will confirm Pooch's assertion about the rattlesnake tail, but every time I strum a G-chord, I think of him and wonder if I'm missing something in today's story.

CHAPTER TWENTY-ONE

A Conversation with Royalty

I am looking for a prince in our hometown. He must be chivalrous, handsome, able to save damsels in distress, and generous to his in-laws. This search stems from a postbirthday conversation with my six-year-old daughter.

A golden opportunity for discovery presented itself when we were in the car with the radio blaring. I turned off the background noise and engaged her.

"Shannon," I asked, "what do you want to be when you grow up? What do you—"

"A princess," she interrupted.

"No, I mean what do you want to *do* when you grow up?"

"I want to be a nurse," she said matter-of-factly.

Her second answer was much more practical. But I could tell her heart was really in the first response.

"Didn't you say you wanted to be a princess first?"

"Yeah."

"Why do you want to be a princess?"

She told me all the things princesses get to wear. Frilly things. Jewelry that costs a lot of money. Princesses also get to ride around in carriages and wave at the little people. Princesses have tea whenever they want and have maids and butlers waiting on them at all hours. Princesses sleep in a soft bed with a canopy overhead. It sounded so good I thought about becoming one myself.

"How do you think you'll get to become a princess?"

She sighed heavily and said, "I guess I'd have to marry a prince."

"Mmmm," I said. "And where do you think you'll find one of those?"

She thought a moment before turning her blue eyes toward me. "Are there any in Bolingbrook?"

Bolingbrook is the hamlet we call home. I haven't seen any castles here, other than the big white one that sells cheeseburgers. I bit my lip and turned to the broken lines of I-355—anything to keep from smiling. She was still looking at me when I turned and said, "I don't know of any, but then I don't know everyone in Bolingbrook."

"They have them in England," she said. "They get to live in castles and things."

"True. But if you moved to England, you wouldn't be able

to see your sisters or brothers. You would be an awfully long way from Mom and Dad, too."

"That's okay," she said. "You guys can come with me."

We ran our errands and stopped by a bookstore. Then we were off to a special restaurant for lunch. Princesses can really put away the chicken fingers and french fries.

We talked about her party the day before. We talked about her friends and her school and her new doll. We talked about the ketchup. We talked about the toll booth and where the money goes when you throw it in. We talked about dessert.

These are things on a princess's mind, so we talked about all of them and kept the radio off.

"Do you want to get married?" I asked.

"Not really," she said. "But I guess I do, because I want to have babies."

The makeup was still faint from her party; blue eye shadow was caked below her brow, a splash of rouge on her cheeks. There were even a few sparkles left from the glittery fingernail polish. Her blond hair was drawn back tightly in a ponytail. She giggled and I could see all those wonderful baby teeth.

You don't have to marry a prince to be a princess, I thought.

CHAPTER TWENTY-TWO

Crinkle, Crinkle, Little Pillow

Not everyone knows I have a favorite pillow, a soft, goose-down creation that sags just right. I wad it up and prop my back against it to read at night. I flatten it out and put my head into the feathery coolness as I go to sleep. Only my wife knows how much it means to me.

One day I climbed into bed and noticed something strange. Andrea had made the bed, and it had that wonderful feeling and smell of clean sheets. But something wasn't right. I grabbed a book and lay down on my favorite pillow. My pillow crackled! I was sickened at the sound. It was soft, but it crackled.

I put my hand against it and squeezed. It crackled some more. *This can't be mine,* I thought. I felt all the pillows under my wife's head, but couldn't find my beloved pillow.

"What's the matter?" she said.

"My pillow. I can't find it."

"It's right there," she said, pointing to the noisy offender. "Under your head."

"That's not my pillow, it's making noises at me."

"Oh," she said, still looking at her magazine, *Today's Christian Pillow Wrecker*, "there were feathers coming out of it and getting all over the room, so I put a pillow guard on it."

"A pillow guard?" It sounded like something left over from the Cold War. Something a communist would sleep on.

"Yeah. It's plastic and it'll keep all the feathers in. I know how much you like that pillow, so I did it for you."

Oh boy, I thought, *that's like drawing earrings on the Mona Lisa! That's like giving someone about to be executed a year's subscription to* Grit*! Thanks a lot, love!*

"Uh, honey," I said very gently, "couldn't we sew it up or something? I mean, to be honest, this really wasn't done for me, it was done for you, right?"

"*We* don't sew. *I* sew. And besides, it won't work. The feathers keep coming out. It's really no different the way it is."

My pulse quickened, but I tried not to get too excited. *I think I can make her understand,* I thought, like the little husband who could. I think I can. She uses word pictures with me; I'll use one with her.

"Honey, you know how much you like doing laundry," I said.

"I hate doing laundry, but I'm the only one who does it."

"Okay, wrong word picture. You know when you're doing the dishes—"

"By the way, I hate doing that, too."

"Right. Okay, I've got it. You know how much you love the feel of clean sheets on a freshly made bed?"

"Yes, and I'm the one—"

"I know you make the bed. That's beside the point. The point is this, what if I were to take these sheets off and put on plastic sheets, how would you like that?"

"Don't be silly. Why would you put plastic sheets on? You haven't had that problem in years."

"No, let's say the mattress leaked feathers or cotton or springs."

"Then I'd go out and get a new mattress."

"Well, suppose you really liked the mattress and you didn't want to get rid of it."

"Why would I get emotionally attached to something I sleep on? If I had the money I'd get a new one."

Frantically I tried to think of another analogy. Gary Smalley can do this in his sleep. But I bet Norma lets him have any pillow he wants. *There must be something I can say to convince her,* I thought.

Before I could come up with anything, she spoke again.

"Look, I know you like that pillow. For whatever reason, it's your favorite pillow. But all the stuffing is coming out of it and going on the bed and all over the room. The vacuum is so heavy I can hardly get it up the stairs, and I'd have to lug the thing up here practically every day to keep it clean.

"If you want to take the plastic guard off and try to sew it, fine. If you can't sew it and you want to go back to the way it was, okay. I'll live with it. But it sure would make it a lot easier if you kept it on there."

She was finished. She had been kind but firm. She had left the door open for me to have my way. I lay back down and it felt like I was sleeping on the *Wall Street Journal*. Every time I rolled over, I felt like I was on the inside of a shopping bag.

Today that pillow represents my commitment to our marriage. Every time I place my head on it, I give up a little of my rights, a little of my freedom, for the greater good of the relationship. When I wake up in the morning I hear the sound as I roll off the pillow, and it reminds me that sometimes you have to sacrifice.

My wife knows I would give my life for her, but she doesn't need that today. Today she needs me to put a plastic thing on my favorite pillow. And by God's grace, I think I can do that.

CHAPTER TWENTY-THREE

———◆———

Cat's in the Cradle, Dad's in the Doghouse

One day Ryan bounced into my home office. I was in the middle of writing some beautiful sentence when I heard, "Hey, Dad, can you change the battery in my car? It doesn't run anymore."

I looked at him like a turtle just waking up from a nap and pointed to the corner. "Just put it over there next to your mother's copy of the *Jane Fonda Lower Body Workout* video. I'll get to it as soon as I can."

"Okay, Dad," he said. He set it down and turned to go. And I was sure I heard him say as he rounded the corner, "Some day I'm gonna grow up to be just like him."

I continued my important work and got lost in whatever I was doing. Maybe I could justify my behavior if I were solving the world's problems. If I were president or a congressman or a doctor saving lives every day, I could make a case for what I did. But I am none of those, and the truth is, there is no reason why I didn't get up right then, retrieve a battery and a screwdriver, and show him how to do it.

But I didn't, and as I turned off the light that night I didn't even notice the car on the floor. I didn't notice it the next day, believe it or not. It was at least four or five days later that I was sitting there, engrossed again in something wildly important, like talking about family values, when I spied my son's toy in the corner. I mentally kicked myself in my mental groin and then mentally screamed and told myself never to do that again. Then I made a mental note to change the battery as soon as I was done.

Somewhere in my desk I have a copy of the *Seven Promises of a Promise Keeper.* Unfortunately one of them is not "I will stay organized," so I can't find the list. "I will replace batteries in remote-control cars" isn't on the list either. At least not specifically spelled out like that.

My days are full of scenarios like this: I'll be reading the paper and my youngest son will toddle up. "Dad?"

"Yeah, Reagan."

"Can aweengareea BOOK?"

"Uh, let me just finish this article here, and I'll read you a book, okay?"

His eyes light up. "Go find one you want to read, and I'll read it as soon as I finish."

I know what will happen next. Because he has such a short attention span, he will go upstairs to get that book and stay there for six weeks playing with his cars. On rare occasions he actually makes it back downstairs with a book. I'll be on to the next article by then and will ask his indulgence. He always gives it, especially when I offer him a snack.

You don't know how bad I feel, lying in bed at night, thinking of all the things I was supposed to do that I didn't.

"Hey, Dad, can you help me with this math problem?"

"Yeah, just wait until I get some gas in the car."

"Dad, can you play ball with me outside?"

"Not now, Son, my spleen is acting up. Maybe tomorrow."

"Dad, what I'd really like is to borrow the car keys. Can I have them, please?"

I asked my wife to comment on my confessions. I said, "What would you include in the list of things I need to confess?" I asked her this while she was cutting out little white snowmen and ironing them on red sweatshirts. Show-off.

"Being in your own world," she said.

"Which means what?" I said.

"You wrote about it; you should know," she said with a tiny bit more bite than I had anticipated. "Being unaware of the world around you. Not following through on the things you say you'll do. Not putting things—"

"Okay, okay, I get the picture! It's only one essay, not the whole book!"

"—away, not hanging things you say you'll hang, not putting your needs ahead of ours."

"And what needs are those?"

"Your need to sleep on a Saturday when I've had the kids all week and you want to rest."

I remembered that Saturday and the look on her face when I said, "I just have to go lie down." I was exhausted from reading the paper and checking e-mail, as I recall it. She looked at me as if I had just announced I was becoming a Nazi.

She was right, of course. (Not about becoming a Nazi.) I don't follow through on everything I say I will do. I commit myself to fixing things just so the requests will stop. My wife lives in our home all day, and little things like working appliances make a difference to her. Not long ago she asked me to fix the coatrack by the door.

"When do you think you can get to that?"

"When do you want me to get to that?"

"I wanted you to get to that before school was out last year, but I don't want to put pressure on you. Why don't you give me a realistic goal when you—"

"Okay, okay," I interrupted, "I'll have it done before school starts."

"That would be wonderful."

And then she did the most terrible thing she could do to

her husband. If there are ladies reading this who wish to inflict pain upon their husbands, remember this tactic: She brought the coatrack that had fallen off the wall and all the tools to fix it and put it just inside the door of my office. On the floor, next to the workout video and the car.

Of course I moved the rack to the upper shelf of my book-case, behind my copy of *Men in Midlife Crisis,* but the damage was done. Every day I saw that coatrack and the sharp screws sticking out the back. The rack hung over me like some black bird of yore.

"When will you fix me?" it said hauntingly. "Nevermore?"

The day before school started I got hives. There is only one thing worse than forgetting to do something you promised to do, and that's remembering it when you have no earthly idea what you are doing. There were already two huge holes where the coatrack had been, and now I was about to make two more. I went on the radio that morning and asked for help from the listening audience. Several callers provided excellent suggestions and at the same time made me feel like a total fool because I didn't understand a word they were saying!

I managed to cut a piece of wood long enough to reach the studs on either end of the coatrack. I attached it to the wall. Then I screwed the coatrack into that piece of wood and tested it by jiggling it up and down. It didn't move. It was a success. It also looked like something installed by Grog the Cro-Magnon carpenter.

Andrea was ecstatic when she saw it. That it was installed in time for school and that it wouldn't fall off again made up for my aesthetic deficiencies. *What a good feeling,* I thought. Why don't I do that more often?

I went into the office and took the car to my son.

"Look," I said. "I'm really sorry I didn't do this the day you brought it to me. You put the screwdriver in here and loosen it, then put the battery in like this."

"Wow, Dad, thanks," he said as the car spun on the kitchen floor.

And you know what? We had a good time then. You know, we had a good time then.

CHAPTER TWENTY-FOUR

My God, Aloha

Our destination was the grandparents' house. Nothing will make you appreciate the psychological effects of modern warfare more than a 550-mile drive over the river and through the woods with seven children. Our first hurdle, however, was the dog.

We did not want to burden our friends with a pup, so we decided on a kennel. Our first choice was full, so we settled on a quaint-sounding place in the country.

"But, Dad," Megan said, "he's so little. He'll be scared."

"No, no," I said. "You've got it wrong. This will be a vacation for him, too. This kennel is like a dog spa, without the heat."

"Really?"

"Yeah. Daily walks around the lawn. Playtime. Wonderful meals. I think they even have nature videos they show a couple of times a day. It's like dog heaven."

I made the mistake of taking the whole family when we dropped off the little ball of fur. We passed one kennel that did look like a dog spa. It sported a finely manicured lawn, a big white house, and a beautiful sign.

"See, the places out here are nice," I said.

"I think he'll be scared of the other dogs," Megan said.

"Nah, there are probably only three or four other dogs there. Besides, he needs the socialization."

After hacking through the brush, we finally found our kennel. A gravel path beside a house led to the canine Shangri-la. But as we pulled closer, the sound of barking became deafening. The children looked in horror as huge dogs lunged at their cages, saliva dripping from their nonmuzzled mouths. I looked at Megan, who was holding pippen. She had that "You're kidding, right?" look on her face. Pippen was excited but calm for his breed. He had no idea what was about to happen.

I looked at my wife. I needed her support. I knew the troops were not going to let pippen enter this sad existence easily. She was laughing so hard her face was red.

"You're not much help," I said through the din.

The next four minutes is a blur. I signed pippen's life away and left him in the care of a grandmotherly woman who said, "I'll put him outside to run."

"Here's his food," I said. But I wasn't sure anyone heard me.

I turned the car around and we passed the kennel, the sound of the barking increasing.

"There he is!" Shannon shouted.

And there was poor pippen, running wild-eyed in front of the cages. He looked almost happy at first.

"Come on, pippen!" the children yelled.

He came loping toward the car, the barking crescendoing to the decibel level of a 747 takeoff. The dogs he passed snacked on bigger things than him. He ran into a wire fence and began flailing wildly. He tried to climb it to get to the people he loved most, but to no avail.

The car was silent for a couple of miles. I tried to lighten the mood and say pretend doggy prayers, but it was no use. Part of us was left in a lonely country cage at the height of flea-and-tick season.

That night we stayed in a hotel with a pool. The mood was somber, and try as we might to exhaust the children, they were wound up by bedtime. I had purposed two rooms in my heart. The older children would stay in a room, and Andrea and I would put the babies to sleep in our room. Then we would have time to talk, play Parcheesi, and do any other thing married people do in hotel rooms, like eat Cheez-Its without sharing.

"Oh honey," she said, not having the same purpose in her heart, "this room is so big, I think we can all fit!"

I took the other room key back to the front desk and said we would only be needing one room. I had purposed that I would be happy with saving money this evening.

Picture the scene: Two adults and seven children in a room built for four. Andrea wedged Kaitlyn into a rickety crib, and the baby immediately began playing with her voice and sucking on her big toes. I had the task of cajoling the next two youngest to sleep. Reagan, who was two at the time, was singing the only three words he could remember from our Vacation Bible School song, "My God, Aloha."

"Okay, we are all going to go to sleep right now, no talking or giggling."

"Waaaaahhhhhh…suck…suck…"

"My God, aloha…"

…laughter about the room…

"And we are not going to go swimming tomorrow if you—"

"…Aloha…my God…"

"Reagan, listen!"

…muffled snickers that break into full-bore laughter about the room…

"Okay, I mean it!"

"…my God…"

"…suck…suck…waaaaahhhhhhhh…"

Andrea was laughing so hard she ran to the bathroom.

"I want it quiet!"

"…aloha…"

Finally Reagan went to sleep, but by then Kristen was having a difficult time. She did not want to be in bed with her little brother or her father, perhaps because the bed kept tipping every time I crawled in. She cried and pulled the covers over her head, woke up her slumbering brother, cried some more, listened to my threats, and finally settled down when I moved between them and put my arms over hers, much like I've seen animal trainers immobilize crocodiles. She breathed deeply and pushed the hair away from her eyes, a telltale sign.

I lay there and listened. I could hear pages turning as the older children read—a wonderful sound. I heard the heavy breathing of my children who had no doubt prayed for their dog before falling asleep. I lifted my head and looked around in the dim light. These faces. These little lives. Gifts from God.

I put my head on the pillow and closed my eyes. I was in that state of near-sleep bliss, where you are aware of things around you but not too aware. Suddenly, somewhere from my left, a head came crashing down on mine, slamming into my ear.

My God, aloha! I thought.

It was Reagan, who was oblivious to his thrashing. In his sleep he was trying to get closer to me. I pushed him farther down in the bed so he wouldn't give me a concussion the next time he turned over, and I went to sleep.

A few days later we headed for home. This time I paid for two rooms and anticipated a dip in the pool, which was bigger than a shelled peanut. We piled into the car and headed toward a nondescript ice-cream shop. Usually I am very conscious of money at places like this. "One small cone, plain. That's it. No, you can't have sprinkles!" But on this night I told the kids they could get anything they wished.

Ryan looked at me with his doe eyes. "Dad, can, can, can, can, can I get one of those, um, um, um, um, you know, those candy bar things in a cup?"

I had just told them they could have anything they wanted.

"Yes," I said, "you can have anything you want." He looked like he had discovered a gold nugget.

"Dad," my oldest daughter said, "can I get a sundae?"

"No. It's too expensive."

"A small one?"

"Oh, okay."

They were as excited as I'd seen them during the entire trip. They were a day away from getting their dog back, a few minutes away from jumping into the pool again, and only seconds away from ice cream. The older kids gathered around the window to place their orders, and I could tell the regulars who visited the shop were curious about our big family.

Reagan and Kristen sat at a picnic table, dutifully waiting their turn, legs swinging back and forth over the asphalt parking lot. Kaitlyn rocked in a car seat beside them. The older children were laughing at some little joke, and Andrea was drinking it all in with them.

Gifts from God, I thought.

In that moment, waiting for a turtle sundae, strawberry-cheesecake yogurt, and a few baby cones, I caught a glimpse of what Jesus must have seen when he pulled a child before his disciples. I saw the future on each face. I saw love. I felt an overwhelming sense of purpose in the midst of the difficulties.

At the same time I felt somehow on the outside of it all. I felt as if this life were going on all around me every day, and I had missed a great deal of it. I had a hundred thousand chances a week to catch this glimpse, but it was so hard to see while I was in the trenches, somebody's head careening toward my left ear.

I don't often cry at ice-cream shops, but I felt a mixture of sadness and hope well within me.

"What are you thinking?" Andrea said as she took a spoonful of her nonfat yogurt.

"Nice night," I sighed.

The kids were laughing around the green table, and people around them were too. Reagan had an ice-cream goatee, and vanilla dripped from his nose. He had a mouth so full of cone he looked like Dizzy Gillespie, and his head bopped back and forth. I doubt anyone else could tell what he was singing, and how perfect the song was.

———◆———

CHAPTER TWENTY-FIVE

The Mundane Song

I live in a place at Mundane and Grace,
Where Life intersects Everyday.
I push and I shove the ones that I love,
And sometimes I can't find my way.

I feel there's a hole down deep in my soul.
I fill it with trinkets and toys.
I long for Your word; Your whisper I've heard,
But I often wind up with just noise.

My deep desire is a mountaintop faith,
Where I see clearly the way.
But You take the common and transform it for
Your use and Your glory each day.

I live in a place at Mundane and Grace,
It's normal to my family.
There's joy and distress, tears, happiness,
And glimmers of glory to see.

I look for the Son in all that is done,
His gifts are right here to receive.
But I stumble, give in; I'm so full of sin,
Each day is a fight to believe.

When will I reach the unreachable goal?
Will I uncover Your will?
Perhaps when my longing is simply for You
My heart will lie peaceful and still.

Some look at this place, a smile on their face.
They laugh at my own private wars.
I just try to see what You've given me.
Each day and forever I'm Yours.

I live in a place at Mundane and Grace,
It's common, what all of us see.
Questions and fears, the answers aren't clear,
But it's right where You want me to be.

Part Two

Mostly Cloudy with a Chance of God

Beware the barrenness of a busy life.

SOCRATES

If you live for the next world,
you get this one in the deal;
but if you live only for this world,
you lose them both.

C. S. LEWIS

CHAPTER TWENTY-SIX

Holy Ground

When I was a child, people said God lived in heaven, and I believed it. So I looked up and tried to find which cloud he was behind. I never saw his face, and since I lived on a farm, I stepped in a lot of things I shouldn't have.

My mother said, "Take off your shoes before you come inside."

That's what life is like. Sincerity leaves your feet messy. I couldn't tell her I was searching for the Almighty in the pasture. If I had, I'd probably be writing this from the Home for Mentally Infirm Farm Boys.

As I grew older, I stopped looking for God. To me, faith became something you believed with all your head. I kept mine down. The notion of God behind the clouds seemed foolish. Childish. So I treated heaven like a metaphor, even though I knew it was real. I asked Jesus into my heart, but my heart had a feeling bypass.

I knew big "God words" and could use them effectively, but they didn't change me. I knew God wanted a relationship with me, but it's difficult relating to someone you never see or hear. You can't even watch God on TV. I strained for his still small voice but heard nothing. Devotions became less like talking with a caring friend and more like stacking cans of tuna. I knew I had to do it, it just wasn't much fun. Going to church and giving an offering was like paying off a divine hit-guy. This was not a relationship; this was holy obligation.

I slowly began to realize that my life's spiritual forecast was not always going to be bright sunshine. On some days it would not even be partly sunny. I saw a holy weatherman standing in front of a map, a low-pressure system going right past his bald head. Superimposed over my day were the words, "Mostly cloudy with a chance of God."

Well, I thought, *at least there's a chance of sunshine.*

With this revelation, I began to crave something deeper, something more than knowledge. I hungered for a belief that could change all of me. I hungered for a really big submarine sandwich. (At times hunger is very practical.) I wanted to stop living for what might be in the future and start living fully right here, right now.

But with this craving came big $10.00 questions. (By the way, these are only $8.97 at Wal-Mart.) Is God really there? Does he care what career I have? In the sovereign plan of the King of the Universe, do I really matter? Is that honey ham? Can I have extra pickles?

These questions, excluding my ravenous thoughts about the sandwich, are like my childhood musings. Some who ask them give up. Others make up their own answers. I want more. I want a God who can break through the everyday clouds.

I remember a time when I would lie on my back, my hands behind my head, and get lost in the bigness of all that was around me. That was last week when I fell asleep in the furniture warehouse. But I also remember sitting in a field and watching the wind brush the clouds past our little part of the world. I remember stars and the sound of crickets.

Life has a way of sapping the stars from your eyes. It has a way of drowning out the wonderful sound of black bugs rubbing their legs together. Fix your eyes on the clouds right now, right where you are. You may find God where you least expect him. And you might want to take off your shoes by the dryer downstairs, because it's here on the cool concrete floor, with stray dog-food pellets and dust bunnies, that you're likely to discover holy ground.

CHAPTER TWENTY-SEVEN

The Bless-You
of Life

Kristen went through her disgruntled nap period when she was three. This is the age at which kids test your parenting acumen by saying "No!" and looking at you like a drill sergeant looks at a whining soldier.

I learned it was important not to ask, "Do you want to take a nap now?" or "Are you ready to take your nap?" This led to a vigorous shaking of the head and a Godzilla-like stomping, complete with bared talons, up the stairs.

I gave her options instead. "Do you want to take a stuffed animal with you for your nap?" "Would you like to take a drink up to your nap, or do you want me to bring it to you after you're covered up?" "Would you care for a sedative with your peanut-butter sandwich?" Such phrases convey the point that a nap is nonnegotiable; only the surrounding conditions are up for grabs.

Age three also ushered in her four-books phase. I would follow her to her room, watching her claw her way up the stairs, and gently tuck her in. She would stick out her hand, hold up three fingers and say, "I want four books." (She takes after her father in math.) Then she would wait to see which four I would pick and demand a favorite tape. I don't know why the number four was so special, she just decided four books in bed was the optimum number. At times I would return to find her on her pillow, both her mouth and book open, curled and twisted in some impossible position around the covers.

Early one morning Kristen and Andrea sat alone at the breakfast table, the shades drawn to block the intensity of the morning sun. It was the time of day when you're not sure about anything. Not even your name. The eyes are puffy. The hair has a mind of its own. They were sitting silently, a couple of cereal bowls between them.

Suddenly Kristen contorted her face and pulled her head back. Andrea looked up, but too late. With all her three-year-old might, Kristen sneezed. She did not have a cold, I'm happy to say, so the sneeze didn't have a devastating effect. Kristen turned from the table and daintily wiped her nose on the sleeve of her Piglet nightshirt.

But she didn't turn back. It was clear there was something drastically wrong.

"What is it, sweetie?" Andrea finally asked.

And then she said the following memorable phrase, which I quote here in its entirety, a phrase which should echo down the halls of kiddom and adultdom alike.

"Mom," Kristen said, "I got bless-you in my Rice Krispies."

She looked down at her bowl, listened to all the snaps, crackles, and pops, and studied the landscape of her breakfast. After a few moments of introspection, she picked up her spoon and, believe it or not, finished the entire bowl. What a trouper.

I would guess that at some point you have gotten bless-you in your Rice Krispies. The cereal bowl of life was fresh and the milk newly poured, and all of a sudden somebody sneezed. When this happens, the bowl doesn't look half as good, and you'd rather just throw it out and start all over again.

So what do you do with the bless-you? A wise person will learn from the three-year-old master: You pick up your spoon and dig in. When somebody hands you a prune, don't throw it away, make lemonade. Wait, that only works with lemons. Okay, make pruneade. When there are no tabs in your life's cassette, stick a piece of tape over the corners and just start recording.

Paul talks about this principle in the book of Romans. The niggling things of life, or even great suffering, develop perseverance. Eventually, perseverance produces in you the thing you want your children to exhibit: character. Character paves the way for hope, which will never disappoint.

It's been a few years since that bless-you scene took place. I

110

can see the fruit already in Kristen's life. She doesn't give up easily. She perseveres, and boy does she have character.

Every time you're tempted to give up, remember this story. Keep going because God promises good things to those who persevere. Character and hope are just around the bless-you corner.

CHAPTER TWENTY-EIGHT

———◆———

Sacrificial Chickens

If you've ever been to a banquet, you know the power of poultry. I believe parachurch organizations would collapse if it weren't for chickens raised on special "banquet farms." This is where they are conditioned to "be tough." When I host such events, I always remember to be thankful for "the chickens who gave their lives for us tonight."

I love being the emcee at these dinners, especially when the speaker is Chuck Colson. This means I get to sit near him, act important, and best of all, hide his forks.

I was at such a banquet not long ago and it was my duty to introduce Mr. Colson. He had unfortunately found someone else's fork but still couldn't locate his napkin (tee-hee-hee), when I stood to welcome the audience.

112

I said a few humorous things that gently warmed the audience for their speaker. Then I put away the list of his accomplishments and accolades and decided to introduce him from my heart. I wanted to express my deep thanks to him. I wanted to say the greatest achievement anyone can have in life is to be known as a friend. Chuck Colson is such a person. He is a friend to the searching politician, to the intellectual, a friend to the prisoner, to the persecuted, a friend to anyone in need. Put aside all the achievements and awards and books. Chuck Colson's greatest legacy is the lives he's touched, and he's touched mine profoundly.

That's what I wanted to say. However, I did not say that because I did not write it down. Remember, I was speaking from my heart, and the heart has a way of saying things that make you want to crawl under the table. What my heart said through my mouth that night was something like, "Chuck Colson's greatest accomplishment in life...is that he's my friend. Please welcome him now."

I felt like pâté! I quickly asked Andrea, "Do you think that introduction came off, well, a little self-serving, that part about Chuck Colson being my friend, I mean, did it sound a bit, like, too self-focused or too—"

"Yes," she said.

"It did?"

"Yes."

Mr. Colson finished speaking about the culture or crime or narcissism or whatever it was. I couldn't concentrate because I was too focused on myself. Then he sat down. I wanted to get back up and make amends for my gaffe. I wanted to say, "You know how I said I was Chuck Colson's friend? Well, it's not true. He hates me! I hid his forks and still have his napkin in my pocket. I'm a big fake." Then I wanted to break down crying.

My heart wanted to do this but my pride, which has veto power over every organ but the large intestine, would not let me do this. I stood up, thanked Mr. Colson, the guests, and the chickens. I even said a nice word about the broccoli.

As I drove home, I thought about the power of celebrity. If I had not wanted to impress Mr. Colson with my warm-hearted introduction, I would have done a much better job. We expect this behavior of teenagers who throng after Holly-wood's latest heartthrob. Voters turn out in droves for their fa-vorite political figure. But I've underestimated the effect of celebrity on me. I'm enamored with big names, adept at elbow rubbing.

I am an evangelical leech, and I'm not proud of it. Some-thing is wrong if I'm judged worthy because of where I sit. Something is wrong if I merely need to have the right connec-tions rather than good ideas or impeccable integrity. The prob-lem compounds when I believe otherwise. Then I begin to gauge individuals on my personal-importance Richter scale in-stead of seeing them as God does.

We all wonder what it would be like to lead a famous per-son to Christ. We dream of clearly explaining the truth of the Bible so the gospel can finally break through. Prayers for the fa-mous become less like evangelism and more like obsession.

I woke up to a startling realization. I rub shoulders every day with people in just as much need as this famous personality. If I really want to be faithful to the message of the gospel, I need to reach out to those who aren't famous, but who are readily available to me every day. If I do that, it won't matter who I'm sitting with, or how hard it is for them to find their hidden forks.

CHAPTER TWENTY-NINE

Ten Seconds

When you live at Mundane and Grace, it's easy to rely on things or events to make life meaningful. A new car, an addition to the house, even resealing your driveway can get your focus off the smallness of daily living.

These things are not bad in themselves, especially if your driveway is cracked, but if you set your affections on them, they become idols. Christmas can be such an event.

Christmas sparkles and replaces drab with shiny. Christmas turns gray into silver and gold. Christmas transforms that wet-earth smell into pine and apple cider. Christmas wrapping and lights make a house a child's playground. The problem is, Christmas is none of these things. These are only outward manifestations of inner joy. If we're not careful, the shiny can replace what ought to be inside.

The best part of Christmas, for parents and children, is not opening presents or enjoying family or even the wonderful music. The best part of Christmas is the anticipation of what's to come. That's why I say you should never open presents on Christmas Eve. The expectant feeling should last until Christmas morning when the pictures are the most embarrassing.

Toy manufacturers know how to create in a child a desperate longing for that Mrs. Potato Head Barbie. Parents know that big spud head with the long, flowing hair will make Christmas truly special. For at least ten minutes.

A writer for the *Focus on the Family Bulletin* put it this way: "If you never allow a child to desire something, she will not fully enjoy the pleasure of receiving it. If you give her a tricycle before she can walk, a bike before she can ride, a car before she can drive…you may actually deprive her of the satisfaction she could receive from those possessions.

"How unfortunate is the child who has never longed for something, dreamed about that prize, or worked hard to get it. Excessive materialism is not only harmful to children, it deprives them of pleasure, too."[1]

God does the same thing at Mundane and Grace. If he gave us all heaven's joys before we longed for it, we wouldn't appreciate the view. If we saw streets of gold in our present condition, we might be tempted to focus on what's under our feet rather than on the Lord of Glory, who inhabits the place.

There are times when God remains silent and lets us wait. Likewise, some of the most important words in our lives are ones we don't say. The pause in a beautiful piece of music is a powerful part of the song, making you long for more, for completion. Silence makes you yearn for things that don't disappoint.

The Israelites waited four hundred years to hear God speak. When his voice finally came, it was the cry of a little child. People longed for the consolation of Israel, for the Messiah. Finally, at just the right time, the Deliverer was born. Sadly, most of Israel missed their Savior.

In the film *Home for the Holidays,* Charles Durning portrays a flawed father speaking to his grown daughter, played by Holly Hunter. She comes home to her dysfunctional family around Christmas and finds herself watching home movies alone with her dad in his paneled basement. Most of this film is forgettable, but this moment caught me unaware.

"Here's what I'm thinking," the father says. "I always settled for less."

"Not true," his daughter says. "Not true."

"I let stuff get in my way. I did it with my work. I did it with my pleasure."

"Dad, please, you don't have to explain."

"Yes I do. Because all of a sudden one day you're sitting in the cellar looking at pictures on the wall, and you think, that wasn't me at all, that was some other guy, some other guy with a smaller waistline dancing with Adelle."

Father and daughter watch the image of a man and woman dancing on the wall.

"Do you remember that day, on the tarmac?" he continues.

"All the kids. Brand new 727 takes off. And when it does she holds on to no one. Eyes wide open."

Durning looks at his daughter. She smiles, trying to remember the moment.

"You were fearless," he says. "Great moment of my life. Great. 1969. Ten seconds tops. I wish I had it all on tape."

And then, almost as powerful as the dialogue, he sits back in his chair and looks out the window, and his daughter looks up at the ceiling, and there is silence.

Fade to black.

Life is made up of ten-second moments just like that one at the airport. The anticipation of a young man, his future, his dreams, dissolve into a memory of a seemingly insignificant moment. He was holding his daughter in his arms watching a plane take off. It wasn't spectacular in any way, yet it held the key to his heart many years later.

We spend our lives waiting for what we think is important only to find that the best things weren't the ones we were waiting for at all. The important things were thrown out like the Christmas wrapping paper. The important things passed us by while we were looking for the TV remote.

Maybe God will be silent today, or perhaps he'll give a spectacular insight. Even if it's only ten seconds, I don't want to miss it.

[1] Dr. James Dobson's *Focus on the Family Bulletin,* vol. 11, no. 9 (October 1998).

CHAPTER THIRTY

On Wings Like Turkeys

Ever want to teach your children a lesson and learn something new yourself? It happened to me one Thanksgiving when my employer provided us with an extra twelve-pound bird. We decided to do the turkey tithe. *If nothing else, this would make Larry Burkett proud,* I thought. My wife had planned to take the older children to a food shelter in the late morning to help serve the hungry and needy. She sees this as a way to expose them to those who are less fortunate.

I had a better plan and questioned whether the shelter would actually need help. "On Thanksgiving and Christmas everyone shows up to help, and then they go away. They need volunteers the rest of the year, but people show up at the holidays because it makes them feel good." Then I added the *coup de fowl,* "Not you of course, dear."

The addendum didn't work. The damage was done. To her credit, Andrea went anyway, later in the day.

The bigger question was not if she would go, but whether she would take our precious over-and-above turkey with her. Andrea had cooked it early in the morning, and it was crisp and brown by ten o'clock. She wanted to donate it to the shelter, but I believed we should do something "local."

"What do you suggest?" my wife asked. "Just go out and find someone who looks turkey deprived?"

"Nobody lives by faith anymore," I said. "If we really believed God, we'd pray he would lead us to the right person, and then we'd take that turkey and give it to them."

Andrea cried that day, though I didn't notice. "It takes every ounce of courage I have just to go to the shelter," she would say later. She felt defeated, but instead of fighting she said, "Okay, let's go."

It was pouring rain as we buckled the kids. The smell of wet leaves and fresh baked turkey filled the air.

"I'm hungry," someone said.

"Quiet kids, we're about to see God work."

I was as expectant as an overdue mother. I was sure something wondrous was about to happen. After all, I was praying to the God who made the sun stand still, who knocked down the walls of Jericho, who calmed the waters on the Sea of Galilee. I wasn't asking for anything close to those things. I was only praying we'd find someone who needed a turkey. This would be a moment my children would never forget. This would be

121

the morning when our God showed himself mighty. We would marvel at his goodness.

The windshield wipers beat to the rhythm of some current Christian tune. A few obstinate leaves clung to the trees, but most were on the ground like a wet blanket. We drove past deserted parking lots and fast-food restaurants. A few cars shared the road with us. Absolutely no one walked the street.

"Dad?" someone called from the backseat. It is the shortest question in the English language which, being interpreted, means, "What in the world are we doing?"

"Pray, kids. I know we're going to find that one person. Look hard now. Don't give up."

We pulled into an apartment complex with its overflowing trash bins. I parked, the rain coming down even harder now, and scanned the rows of curtained windows. Nothing. Just the sound of the rain and the radio. I turned it off, half expecting someone to tap on the window and ask, "Sir, can you help a poor man find some food?"

A still, small voice broke the silence.

"Dad, there's nobody here."

"There's somebody in this world who needs a turkey today, and we're going to find that person," I said resolutely. "This turkey has somebody's name on it, we just don't know who it is."

Aimlessly we roamed, driving through foreign neighborhoods and alleys.

"How are they going to get the turkey home if it's raining so hard?" someone else asked.

"Maybe we'll give them a ride," I said.

"Dad, there's no more room. We take up all the seats."

"Are there no Joshuas or Calebs in this car?" I said. "You guys are worse than the children of Israel. You just wait and see."

But it was like waiting for the Great Pumpkin to rise from the patch. God had provided the ram in the thicket for Abraham. I had provided the turkey in the pan. But where was Isaac or whoever was supposed to eat it?

Andrea looked at me and tried to smile. "Let me take it to the shelter, I'm sure they can use it. You go home and watch the game."

The game. I forgot about the game.

It felt like failure, but sometimes faith feels that way. Sometimes the right thing means obeying the call you've already been given, even if it wasn't your idea. Sometimes faith doesn't make you feel as good as you want. Faith can make you mount up with turkey wings.

I'm not sure my kids remember our fruitless search that day, but they have wonderful stories of serving hungry people and how thankful those at the shelter were for their help. I looked at Andrea's face later as we sat down to eat our own meal. There was satisfaction in it, as if a stone had been rolled away.

"How do you like your turkey?" she asked, wondering whether to serve me dark or white meat.

"Well done," I said. "Well done."

CHAPTER THIRTY-ONE

You Gotta Hold the Baby Even When She Spits

Fistfights break out whenever we bring a baby home for the first time. It happens every time. As soon as Andrea gets in the door with the tightly wrapped child, little voices call out, "I want to hold her! I want to hold her!"

I'm a lot more lenient than I used to be. With our first baby you had to have a graduate degree in child development just to pull the blanket off her face. Now with seven kids, someone at the grocery store will smile and I'll hand the bundle over like a twenty-nine-cent can of pork and beans.

Still, with very tiny hands begging to hold the new one, you have to be careful. There is wisdom in supervising the holding experience. You sit and place a hand under the baby's neck and tell your daughter what a wonderful mommy she will make some day. Secretly you hope to get the baby back with its spinal column intact.

"That's it, sweetie, now hold her snug but not too tight. There you go. Whoops! Ha-ha—not that tight, let's give her a little oxygen now. When she turns those funny colors it means you need to hold her softer. There. Good. Okay, now if you'll put your hand right here behind her head, it won't swing back and forth along the ground. That's it. Good girl!"

Our children have been quick learners, so the following story should not deter you from asking them to baby-sit, should you have the opportunity. In order to protect her identity, I will refer to the offending child as "Sibling."

Sibling wanted to hold the baby when Kaitlyn was only a few weeks old. Kaitlyn was dressed in a pink infant dress, and what little hair she had was coiffured with a matching ribbon. She was adorable. This no doubt added to Sibling's desire of holding such a living doll.

Sibling lovingly cradled little Kaitlyn in her arms and said sweet things to her. I turned my back for a second. The next thing I knew, little Kaitlyn was bouncing on the floor. Thank God for thick carpeting and Stainmaster. I picked her up and calmed her, then looked at her astonished Sibling.

"What happened?" I said.

"She spit on me!" Sibling said, as if this kind of thing never happens.

I helped Sibling clean her own pretty dress and said, "It's

125

important to remember: You gotta hold the baby even when she spits."

She frowned and went into another room, leaving me to ponder my own lesson. Life looks so wonderful from our limited viewpoint. When we're young, it's fluffy and pink and we can't imagine it will taste like anything other than cotton candy. We dream of "what could be," forget "what might be," and take hold with both hands. On the way to "what will be," "what is" starts tasting less like candy and more like Pepto-Bismol. Then life spits up. As it grows older, life spits up *and* kicks us in the teeth, and we're occasionally tempted just to drop the whole thing.

But the more life you live, the more you love it, and even when it's bad you learn to not let go. The spitting and kicking make the other parts that much more enjoyable.

If this is your life, remember that spitting lasts for a season, but joy comes in the morning. That's sort of in the Bible. And if you ever drop the baby, pick it up and hang on. There's a Father who loves you in spite of it all.

CHAPTER THIRTY-TWO

The Eye of the Storm

S unday morning at our house is a little like Dante's *Inferno.*
A great lament goes up among the children when they discover someone else has gone before them into the water chamber. In a few moments I will hear the hum of hair dryers and the shouts of, "Has anybody seen my brush?" I will hear a squeal of discovery, and then the one using the hair dryer will say, "I couldn't find mine. Why can't I use it? Come on, give it back!"

Some of the children wake early and get dressed immediately. They avoid the chaos, get dressed, and head for breakfast, where Pop-Tarts have been lovingly removed from their box and wait to be consumed. These are my favorite children. They are altogether lovely offspring who do not fight me for the solitary joy of a shower.

In a few moments I will need to pull the covers off one of my daughters, grasp her by the ankles, and pull her from the warmth of her bed. This is the only way she will be on time, and she will not look at me without scowling until after church.

In a few moments everyone will gather around the door of the sacred living-room closet, the one I keep repairing. It has taken so much abuse from the Sunday maelstrom that it has fallen off its hinges several times. I've drilled and filled so many holes in this door that it now has the consistency of cheese. They will gather here, like cows at a trough much too small, and dig for their shoes. The little ones stand at the edges and wait for theirs to come flying past.

And then we will endure perhaps the most difficult part of the morning. Realizing we are late and sensing the tension mount as my wife asks, "Has anyone seen the diaper bag?" I venture outside to move the car into position for takeoff. This is one of only three moments of peace I experience before the prelude to worship. Moving my car with no one around and writing the check to put in the offering are two things I do alone.

Making sure the dog is inside and the back door is indeed locked, I follow the straggling children to the car, yell at the one upstairs to hurry up on pain of being left behind, and prepare for the battle.

"Mom, you said I could sit in front!"

"She always gets to sit up there, why can't I?"

"I don't want to sit by him!"

"Mom, you told me last week I could sit in the middle."

"Aaaaaaaaaaahhhhhhh! My Pop-Tart!"

"Pick it up, it's not that dirty."

"Aaaaaaaaaaahhhhhhh!"

"Do I have to ride in the way-back again?"

"This car is dirty!"

"Hey, you're the only ones who ride back there."

"He hit me!"

"Don't hit him back, it'll only make things—"

"Wahhhhhhhhh!"

"—worse."

"Well if you're not going to eat it, I will!"

"Aaaaaaaaaaahhhhhhh! He's eating my Pop-Tart!"

"You're on my seat belt. Get off!"

Praise God, from whom all blessings flow.

"Is everybody buckled?"

"Can you turn a tape on, Dad?"

"Wait, I forgot my Bible. Don't back out yet, Dad. Please?"

"Okay, but hurry up."

"I can't get out."

"Just climb over her. But watch the—"

"Aaaaaaaaaaahhhhhhh!"

"—Pop-Tart."

"Dad, I can't get in. The door's locked."

"Honey, while you're in there, could you get the baby wipes? I forgot them again."

Praise him, all creatures here below.

"Dad, pippen sounds like he really needs to go outside."

"No, come on. Get in the car."

(Singing): "I know a song that gets on people's nerves, gets on people's nerves, gets on people's nerves..."

"Wait, Dad, I'm not buckled!"

"We're late! Just hurry up."

(Singing): "I know a song that gets on people's nerves, and this is how it goes..."

"Oh no!"

"What is it now?"

"I forgot my memory verse."

"You always forget your memory verse."

"I do not!"

Whack.

"Wahhhhhhhhh! He hit me!"

"I don't think the verse would've helped."

(Singing): "I know a song that gets on people's nerves..."

(In unison): "SHUT UP!"

"See, I told you it would get on your nerves."

Praise him above, ye heavenly host.

"I don't want to go to church."

"I don't want to go to the nursery."

"I have to go to the bathroom."

"Why didn't you go *before* we left the house?"

"Because I couldn't find my shoes."

"What? That doesn't make sense."

"Dad, hurry up. I can tell she really has to go."

"I'm going as fast as I can. Just think of something else."

"Dad, are you teaching Sunday school today?"

"Oh no. I forgot the Sunday school stuff."

"Mommy, can I sit beside you in the service?"

"No, we are not going to have another scene about who gets to sit by Mommy."

"Can I hold Kaitlyn when we get there?"

"Mom, you said I could hold her!"

(Singing): "I know a song that—"

(In unison): "SHUT UP!"

Praise Father, Son, and Holy Ghost.

"Okay, somebody take her to the bathroom, and the rest of you go with your mother. I'll park the car."

"I hate being late."

"I don't want to go to church."

"I can't unbuckle!"

"No, you have to leave your Pop-Tart here."

"Wahhhhhhhhh!"

"Look, I'll leave it right here on the wheel well for when you get back."

They pass through the doors and I park the car. This is my third solitary moment of the morning. I turn off the engine and collect myself. Church is my eye of the storm. On both sides is a hurricane, but when we're all inside the storm calms.

Breathe, I tell myself. *Don't forget to breathe. Pretty soon this will all be over and you'll be gumming oatmeal and wishing you could do it all over again.*

I follow the Pop-Tart crumbs inside and wish there were some way to commemorate these days. The children of Israel used to erect stones at strategic places so they would remember the faithfulness of God. If it were lawful, I'd put a bunch right here where I let the kids out.

Someone hands me a bulletin and shakes my hand, and I see the little ones in the front row. Like the Gadarene demoniac the kids are all dressed and in their right minds. No one fights for position. No one sings annoying songs. As the music begins, I sit down and worship the God who parted the Red Sea, shook the walls of Jericho, and got my family here in one piece.

Which one is the bigger miracle?

Amen.

—◆—

CHAPTER THIRTY-THREE

Changing Your Teeter-Totter

We were driving home from church one Sunday when Shannon asked from the backseat, "Dad, what's another word for *stubborn?*"

The first word I said was *intractable.* The first word I thought of was *Kristen.* When Kristen gets an idea in her little head, it takes nothing short of an act of Congress to get it out.

"Can stubborn be a good thing?" Shannon asked.

"Yes," I said. "There's such a thing as stubborn love."

As we talked about the word *stubborn,* I recalled one particularly challenging Sunday morning when Kristen was obstinate cubed. She was up late the night before working on her "benny tell," which is how she says the word "ponytail." She is too young to understand the words "late for church," so she pranced about her room Sunday morning, oblivious to her parents' pleas.

Six other children were in the car, waiting.

"You're not going to get a Pop-Tart if you don't come now!" someone coaxed to no avail.

Andrea finally tromped down the stairs like a defeated soldier. She looked at me, shook her head, clearly vowing not to return to Kristen's room.

"Don't leave me alone with it!" I begged, but Andrea was already out the door. It was just me and the demon child.

"Kristen," I called, "we have to go. You're going to wear what you have on right now, no matter what it is. Here I come."

"I wanna teeter-totter," she said as I entered her room.

She looked straight at the floor, her arms crossed against her bare chest. She wore only the prayers of her siblings and a pair of Little Mermaid panties.

"Kristen, we can go to the park this afternoon. We don't have time for a teeter-totter right now. We have to go to church."

"I want the teeter-totter."

I heard the door bang downstairs, and the familiar swish of my wife's clothes.

"She wants a teeter-totter," I yelled from the room. "What is she talking about?"

Andrea laughed. "A leotard," she said. "She wants to wear her black leotard."

"She can't wear that. She'll freeze to death!"

"Okay," Andrea said, "I'll be in the car."

Kristen was holding the teeter-totter when I turned toward her. She pointed toward her dresser and asked for a pair of tights.

"We don't wear a leotard to church," I said. "It's not right."

"Why not?"

"I don't know, it's one of the commandments, I think. Now let's find you something else."

"I wanna wear the teeter-totter."

"You can't," I said, opening the only drawer she calls her own, the bottom one. Her clothes were wrapped together like a hundred wrinkled worms. "Wear this," I said, handing her the first outfit I found.

She looked away like I was holding a dead chicken. A horn honked. It was a bad sign because it meant either Andrea was fed up with waiting or the other kids had declared mutiny.

I'm sure experts have effective techniques for this parenting challenge. There is probably a wonderful verbal approach that could have extricated me from this tight spot. But at that moment I knew why God had allowed me to watch Big Time Wrestling as a youngster. I managed to get her in a shirt and some pants. Then I put her over my shoulder while I struggled to find matching socks and retain my hearing simultaneously. I carried her down the steps upside down as she wailed and clawed for the handrail. I bent down to get her shoes from the closet. This was a mistake. Somewhere in my head I heard,

"Use your legs," but I bent wrong and the unspeakable happened.

My back. Ow!!!

I let out a piercing scream as I sat down on the nearest chair. I located the socks Kristen had kicked off, and then I Velcroed her shoes as tightly as I could. I didn't want to stand with her in my arms and risk more damage, but I also didn't want her to get those shoes off, so I bit down on the inside of my cheek until I could taste blood and picked her up and flew out the door. As I strapped Kristen into the car seat, I noticed I had knocked her "benny tell" out, but there was no turning back now.

On we drove. When we pulled into the church parking lot, pain shot through my body and I doubted I could sit in a folding chair for a whole service. It felt like someone had stuck a rusty ice pick through my lower back and was turning it.

Andrea and the other kids jumped out and made a mad dash before I could protest. Again it was just Kristen and me. I hobbled out and opened her door. She was still buckled, so I thought we would have a talk.

"Kristen, I'm sorry you couldn't wear your leotard to church. You can put it back on when you get home, if you like."

I unbuckled her and she looked for the others, but they were now inside the doors. I put my hands under her arms and she relaxed. I carefully lifted her from the car seat and put her down; she stood by the car diligently waiting as I closed the door.

Then she took my hand in hers so easily I nearly missed it. She skipped along and looked up with her stubby-tooth smile, as if the preceding twenty minutes had never happened. This is forgiveness, I thought, *sweet and bouncy.* I regretted, only for a moment, that she wasn't wearing that black teeter-totter. I don't think it would have offended God a bit.

CHAPTER THIRTY-FOUR

Wiping the Sleep from My Soul

This morning I woke up exactly five minutes before my alarm rang. Because I work in morning radio, it was mind-numbingly early. My wife was sleeping, as she usually does, on her side with a pillow over her head. I heard Kaitlyn's gentle breathing from her crib on the other side of the room. The rest of the house was quiet and dark.

I fumbled for my watch on the nightstand, pulled it close, and pressed the light button. My watch sports the word *Illuminator*, which I think is really cool. The bluish light flashed 3:25. Five measly minutes before I had to get out of bed. I've awakened in the middle of the night before. I usually look at the clock and think, *Oh well. I have another two hours, or another hour.* Then I go back to sleep.

My first conscious thought this morning was, *What am I gonna do with five minutes?* I checked again, just to make sure, and I was right, only now it was 3:26 and I'd wasted a full minute.

I couldn't remember any of my dreams, couldn't figure out what day it was. I was just up, and I only had four minutes before my feet hit the floor.

Isn't it supposed to be good that you wake up just before your alarm? I wondered. *I've heard it means you're getting enough sleep, so that's a positive, not a negative. Boy, you're really tough on yourself for this early in the morning.*

I looked at my watch again. One minute left. I could have been praising God for the last four minutes. I bet Chuck Swindoll doesn't wake up like this. Or Max Lucado. I bet they wake up reciting the entire book of Philippians or singing the third verse of "Wonderful Grace of Jesus." Everybody knows the first two verses; it's that third one that separates the spiritual giants from the regular people like me.

What a pitiful life. I need help.

I turned off the alarm before it rang and quietly got ready for work. I jumped in the car, grabbed a newspaper at the corner stand, and flipped on the radio, the cobwebs still clinging to my brain. The first song I heard was "Praise to the Lord, the Almighty."

When they got to the last verse, the one that says, "Praise to the Lord, O let all that is in me adore him," I wished that had

139

been my first thought of the morning, rather than being depressed about waking up five minutes early.

"All that hath life and breath, come now with praises before him."

Hey, that's me. I have breath. As a matter of fact, that would make a pretty good advertisement for Christianity. Instead of the Got Milk? campaign, we should say, Got Breath? Praise God!

"Let the amen sound from his people again."

Yeah, I want to sound an amen again.

All these wonderful thoughts began to transform my sullied day. But then, instead of singing, "Gladly for aye we adore HIM," which is how the song was written, the group on the radio sang, "Gladly forever adore him." And they didn't stop there. They sang, "Gladly forever and ever and ever adore him," which is not just changing "aye" to make it understandable; it gets really close to gall if you ask me.

Then the song was over and I realized I had missed it. I didn't focus properly on the ending because I was thinking about someone changing "aye" to "forever and ever and ever."

Thus began a day of searching, of realizing I am a thirsty, desperate soul. I'm looking for love, comfort, peace, hope, joy, fulfillment, and a warm fuzzy feeling every week or two. I really, *really* want God's benefits. But I'm not enthused about the pain associated with obtaining these spiritual by-products. I want a touch from the living God on my own terms.

I know that Jesus is in my heart...but sometimes I don't feel like he's there. It feels like there might possibly be someone hid-ing behind my spleen, or maybe sleeping near my pancreas, but I'm not sure. Sometimes my life feels ineffective and God seems distant, almost uncaring. He may seem close during a particularly eventful Sunday or a moving seminar, but he's not involved in the daily grind.

My problem is not a lack of materials. I have forty versions of the Bible, a myriad of commentaries, books by the ton, Christian music in every conceivable style, scores of devotionals by preachers, teachers, and conference speakers. I can watch Christian television, hear Christian radio, consult my Christian nutritionist or my Christian psychologist, and compare their advice with my Christian fitness expert. I can use Christian computer programs and even wear Christian clothes. With all of this at my disposal, God still seems faraway. Why?

The answer came as I was changing lanes behind a huge truck. Maybe I haven't really been looking for God after all.

I thought about it a few minutes. If I haven't been looking for God, what have I been looking for? An experience? A revelation? And if what I truly crave *is* God, how do I find him in the midst of my everyday life? Even at 3:25 A.M.?

In *My Utmost for His Highest,* Oswald Chambers writes about the difference between God and what we long for. Jesus had taken his disciples to a high mountain and showed them great things. They wanted to stay, but Christ would not let them.

Chambers writes: "We see His glory on the mount, but we never live for His glory there. It is in the sphere of humiliation that we find our true worth to God, that is where our faithfulness is revealed."[1]

As I pulled behind the truck I realized the "sphere of humiliation" is my entire life, and if this truly is where my faithfulness is revealed, if this is where God is today, then it's right where I need to be.

Aye?

[1] Oswald Chambers, *My Utmost for His Highest* (New York: Dodd, Mead & Co., 1935), 204.

CHAPTER THIRTY-FIVE

Thankfulness from a Four-Year-Old's Perspective

I want to be as thankful as a little child today, so I'm going to go into the world of a four-year-old girl.

When you're a girl and you're four, you're thankful for hats. For scarves and tiny necklaces. For frilly dresses, puffed sleeves, and white socks you can roll up. You're thankful for shoes with Minnie Mouse on the outside so you can tell which one to put on which foot. For underwear with little pictures on the front, so you can tell which holes to put your feet in. For the thought, *Hey, I don't have to wear diapers anymore.* And for the feeling that, all of a sudden, you're growing up.

As a four-year-old girl, you're thankful for makeup. Nail

polish. Blush. Eyeliner. Four-year-olds are also thankful for their mom's clothes. For mom's shoes and hose and skirts and dresses that make you feel big, even though you're still in a little-girl world. There is a feeling of safety as you lumber around and trip over the long dress.

If you're a tomboy, you don't really care for the frilly dresses, puffed sleeves, and makeup. You're thankful for frogs and bugs and easy-to-climb low-hanging tree limbs. You're thankful for a smooth handle on your dad's shovel. You're thankful for a yard to dig holes in and for worms and ants and ladybugs.

When you're four, you're thankful for food. Except when your parents order Chinese and ask you to eat chicken-fried rice and your dad has to pick out all the little chicken pieces. When you're four, you don't really care if a chicken has given its life for you. If you don't like it, you don't like it. But you don't have to be consistent when you're four. You can say you don't like chicken and then order chicken nuggets at a restaurant and gobble them down without a thought of the inconsistency.

When you're four you pray, "Thank you for this food. Thank you that we could go outside today and play. Thank you that we're not having chicken tonight." A four-year-old's prayers get right to the point. They don't dance around with big words or platitudes. "Help Grandma's gall bladder to get better. Amen." That's all you need when you're four.

When you're four and you like cheese, you can eat it all day and not think a thing about what it's doing to your body. When you're four, the four best words in the day might just be "peanut butter and jelly."

When you're four you don't worry about mortgages. You don't have a lot of anxiety about anything except where you put your doll dress or where your Sunday-school paper went. Last week they covered Saul in Sunday school. Saul, in my four-year-old's mind, is totally green. And the green goes outside the lines, but there's no anxiety about that, because coloring is the point. When you're four, you're thankful for crayons. You don't have to have 128 of them to be thankful. But when you do have 128, with all the points still on and none of them broken and you don't have to share any with your little brother, life is good. Almost as good as being the first person to put your spoon in the new jar of peanut butter, or riding where you want in the car (by the window) and feeling the wind blow through your hair so you can close your eyes and pretend you're flying upside down in your own airplane, or having a bunch of people to bring you peanut-butter sandwiches with all the crusts cut off and brand-new crayons when you break one.

When you're four and it's sunny outside, and you've got your Minnie Mouse shoes on the right feet, a clean dress or jeans and a crayon or two, a swing set in the backyard and a Barbie Bike with training wheels, life is grand.

145

Now if you can just get Mom to rethink that chicken casserole.

Dear God, teach me today to be thankful for the great and small in my life. Amen.

CHAPTER THIRTY-SIX

I Didn't Even Know Her Name

Our youth pastor did an unscientific survey of some teenagers and asked them a provocative question. If Jesus came to a high school, what group would he hang out with? Would it be the geeks? The jocks? The druggies? The religious kids? It was nearly unanimous. The kids thought if Jesus came to their school, he would hang around with the Christian kids who carry their Bibles and wear the Christian jewelry and T-shirts.

Jesus' choice of associates shocked the religious establishment of his day. They accused him of terrible things simply because he tried to reach those who needed him most. In Mark 2 Jesus answered the question of why he was often seen with sinners and tax collectors. "It is not the healthy who need a doctor, but the sick. I have not come to call the righteous, but sinners."

I'm glad Jesus did this, but I can't say it's a pattern in my own life. I've surrounded myself with people who are like me, people who sin in private but not in public, people who look good on the outside.

The problem with mingling with outwardly sinful people is that life gets dirty. Some people smell like smoke. Some people get drunk. Some people tell dirty jokes that are hard not to laugh at, so it's easier to distance ourselves from them and keep things tidy, at least on the surface.

But Jesus didn't come in the name of tidiness. He came for messy people with messy lives and loads of sin. He came for people who make me feel uncomfortable. These are the people I want to judge. But take away the smoke and some jokes, and I'm just like them. I'm actually worse, because I think I'm better than them.

A few years ago a fire destroyed the Paxton Hotel in downtown Chicago. Those of us in the suburbs watched the news and felt badly for the victims and their families, but a couple of days later we tired of the investigation. I work a few blocks from the hotel and watched the fire engines and the snarled traffic from my office window. The grim search for bodies was unsettling.

A day or two later I began to think about her. I didn't know her name. She didn't show up every day or even every week, but she was a fixture in our lobby.

She wore long pullover sweaters and polyester pants that swished when she walked. Her matted hair, once dark, was turning gray. Her shoes were held together by threads and a prayer. It seemed her only friend was the coat she wore in every season, even in the dead of summer.

Her most distinguishing feature was her voice. When she talked, you could hear the sound reverberate off the high ceiling and through the elevator shaft. Often she talked to herself. She laughed.

At times she scared me. Her eyes were piercing brown. Once I was on the elevator with about fifteen elderly visitors. She stepped on at the lower level, and we were shoved close together. I held my breath.

She panned the crowd of stooped and withering men and women and quoted her *King James Version* of the Bible.

"Looks like we've got a bunch of hoary heads," she cackled. "That means white head."

I smiled to those around us, hoping they would understand this was not an employee but an intruder. She laughed again loudly and shook her head. The people didn't seem to mind.

I remember walking in one day and seeing her sitting at the entrance by the elevators. I passed her quickly, pushed the "up" button, and darted toward the water fountain around the corner. I stayed there until the familiar ding of the elevator bell signaled my deliverance. I stepped through the door and turned around to see her talking and laughing. The room was empty except for the receptionist. The woman talked to the wall.

When the door closed, I rolled my eyes and sighed. I had dodged her again.

I was thinking about these moments when a coworker stepped into my office. I mentioned this lady and asked if he knew her. "Sure," he said. "She comes to our church. She's always asking the receptionist about her makeup. Says she can't do a thing with her hair." And then he said the words that made my heart sink. "I heard she was living at the Paxton."

His phone rang and he left me staring out the window. She was living at the Paxton?

"I didn't even know her name," I said out loud.

We are all a little crazy, I thought. There probably isn't much difference between what goes on in my head and what came from her mouth. She was just different.

God left me here in the midst of messy people's lives for a purpose. Too often I'm just concerned about myself. If I could ride the elevator with her again or see her in the corner staring out the window, I believe I would treat her more kindly. Maybe I'll have the chance today to meet someone like her. Maybe then I'll get it right and ask her name.

CHAPTER THIRTY-SEVEN

Ki Go Living

With Batman on his chest and a black cape on his back, my son is an unlikely theologian. Besides, his eyes are too wide. You have to wear little spectacles and look erudite to be a true theologian. He's short, only a couple of feet tall, and he gives a blank stare when I bring up names like Calvin, Zwingli, or Luther. He is two. But the lessons he gives have stayed with me longer than those from just about any published author.

Today's lesson concerns a wild dependence upon God, something I lost along the way. Early in my Christian life I felt a certain abandon, a lust for the spiritual. I wanted special access and special answers to my prayers. All this was fine for a while, until my desires changed and I decided to be practical. I settled for realism in my spiritual journey. I settled for less. Enter Batman theologian.

He was there one day as I put on my shoes and reached for

the door. He was just learning to talk. Before I had time to slip away, a little voice behind me said, "Ki go?"

"Oh, hi buddy, I'm going to drop something in the mail-box."

"Ki go?"

"No, I'm just going to the mailbox. You stay here."

He looked hurt. "Ki go?" he whined.

An hour later I was ready to retrieve his big brother at soccer practice. "I'll be right back," I yelled to the house, hoping someone who cared would hear me.

From a room upstairs I heard pounding on the carpet. *Bong, bong, bong, bong.* Batman again at the top of the stairs.

"Ki go?" he called down.

No matter what the occasion—a trip to the store, a walk to the park or the library—Batman is willing and anxious to go. He doesn't care what I'm doing. He doesn't mind if I'm not focusing on him as we head toward my important destination. All he wants is my presence. "Can I go?" he says in his own two-year-old way.

The first time he said it, it took me a few moments to understand. Now I expect the words any time I'm going away.

We were in the grocery store in the cheese section, with Batman in the child seat facing me. I pushed, focusing on the task at hand, frustrated with the slowness of other shoppers. Only inches from my face, the same voice sang: "I'm so happy in Jesus, every day."

I looked at him and stopped the cart. "Yeah, I guess you're right," I said.

Lately I've come to believe this is why God didn't give me a special pipeline or a positive answer to my early prayers. God has given this lump of flesh in a black-and-gold costume right when I needed it.

My previous goal was the spiritual mountaintop and a palpable touch from God. Today I have a new prayer: "God, I don't care where you take me. I don't care where you're going. I just want to be with you. Your agenda is my agenda. Your focus in mine. I'll go wherever you go, and I'll be happy in whatever journey you provide."

I should be honest and tell you there is one place Reagan has trouble with this principle. Naps. After lunch he climbs the stairs behind me, slump shouldered. I've been bringing him to my bed with his little sleeping bag and letting him rest while I read a book. He thrashes, swings his legs over the side, gets pulled back, cries, wipes his eyes, and turns over. Before long his eyelids are heavy and I hear the rising and falling of his little lungs like waves on the seashore. Batman is in a place he didn't want to be, but he is still at rest.

Even asleep, a good theologian can teach valuable lessons.

CHAPTER THIRTY-EIGHT

The Hardest Lesson of Camp

I never went to camp when I was a kid. I never knew what it was like to be left alone and watch your family drive away, except for the times they got fed up with me and took me to Kmart and left me in automotive for a few hours.

But you know what? I'm experiencing that feeling now, vicariously, and it's much harder on this side. It's harder letting go, saying good-bye, and watching this little bundle you brought home from the hospital, all helpless and pink, run toward a camp counselor you've never seen before.

Oh, I hope it's not the counselor with the ring through her forehead.

I have a picture of my daughters on my desk at work. The youngest was two at the time, and she sat with her sisters on a table at one of those mall picture galleries. She wore her frilly dress, and the photographer had placed her hands together in front of her. It's what I call her "Cosette" pose from *Les Misérables*. That's the Cosette after she grew up and got away from the innkeepers, the Ternardiers, who made her play with sticks in the corner and eat moldy bread.

Anyway, when I look at her in this dress, with her hands folded, her chubby cheeks, and those tired eyes, I'm reminded of the days when I could get her to do anything I wanted just by threatening to take away her blanket. But I can't do that anymore because she's growing up. When she headed for camp, she even left her blanket at home.

I wrote a letter to our camper this week that said we weren't doing very well in her absence. I told her we were all so sick no one could eat anything, except for her younger brother, who was eating everything! I told her tears were flooding her bedroom, that her mother was moping around like someone had stolen her barrel of monkeys.

I told her I went outside that morning, the sun just peeking over the horizon, a few clouds rolling by, and I thought about her in her bunk. Would the light wake her? Would she open her eyes and think of her family as she listened to the birds outside her cabin door? Or would somebody come in and slip a frog into her sleeping bag? Was there an ache in her soul for home?

The best part of camp for me is Friday. I get to be the hero, riding in on my silver horse, Festiva, and whisking her away from all she's known for a week.

Then comes the most difficult realization. The hardest part of camp is not the letting go at the start, it's the letting go at the end, when she sees there's more to life than our four walls, when her world opens up and she realizes, maybe for the first time, that leaving Mom and Dad isn't all that bad. She can make it. For a week, to begin with, then for a summer, and then...

I wonder, does God ever look at me this way? How hard is it for him to watch me leave and forget about my real home and what's waiting for me there? Who thinks of me in the morning?

Camp is the first wing flap out of the nest. It's the first time our daughter has been out on her own, trusting in herself and in God. I would rather love her by choosing for her, but that's not true love. This is the hardest part of this week for me.

If you don't count the laundry.

CHAPTER THIRTY-NINE

Conversations with My Shirt

To confirm their faith, some look for a code in the Bible; others look for pieces of the ark on Ararat. I found God's voice in a shirt. Sort of.

The event came at a crucial time in my life. I was trying to make some important decisions. I had been praying for some sign, some special word from God about direction. I would have taken a message in the clouds or sacred guidance spelled out in my taco salad. I wanted something as dramatic as the Shroud of Turin or a weeping computer screen.

I got a holey shirt.

I was doing a load of wash when I came upon a T-shirt from college. I had rescued it from Andrea's numerous attempts to trash it or give it to charity. The holes in the shirt, when held up to the side of the dryer, seemed to be saying something.

(At this point you are to suspend disbelief while I use a fictional situation to make an important spiritual point. Thank you for your cooperation.)

"Did you say something?" I asked the shirt.

Nothing.

"Come on, I need some help here. What did you say?"

"Okay," the shirt said with a gravelly voice, "take me into your office, and I will show you."

This blows the whole mundane thing out of the water, I thought. I've got my next book in my hands right here. *Conversations with My Shirt.*

I ran to my office and held the shirt up so it could have a look around. This was not just a holey shirt, it was wholly holey. I held it in midair until it spoke again.

"You have heard that there are hidden meanings behind the Hebrew letters in the Old Testament, right?"

"Hey, you're a pretty smart shirt," I said.

"Shut up."

"Okay, yes, I've heard something about it, but I haven't really read that much."

"I am a shirt that will help you search the hidden meanings found in any book."

"Really?" I said, picking one off the shelf. "Even this hymnal?"

"No. I only do red hymnals edited by Donald Hustad."

"I see," I said, finding *Hymns for the Living Church.*

"Open it to any page and you will see."

I opened to page 286, "Years I Spent in Vanity and Pride." I laid the shirt over the page carefully.

"Now ask me a question," the shirt said.

"Okay, should I finish doing the laundry?"

I looked through the holes and read, "I trembled... gladly...knowing only pardon. My...liberty."

"Wow," I said, "I think this means I don't have to do laundry."

"Just wait until you start reading the Bible with me," the shirt said. "The Ten Commandments are really fun. I can answer all your questions about God's will and your future."

From somewhere inside me a still, small voice whispered caution. There was suddenly something sinister about a talking shirt that interpreted Scripture. I felt uneasy.

"I know what you're thinking, but try it," the shirt said reassuringly. "Go ahead and try me once. Just ask a question, and I'll give you the inspired answer."

Andrea walked in at that moment and I realized my mistake. I had been asking God for a divine crystal ball. I didn't want to get to know God through his Word; I wanted a holy holey shirt to speak to me directly. I wanted to break God's code and receive a splash of heaven, lights and visions and specifics for my life. He wanted to put his code on my heart. I wanted to know the plan. He wanted me to know him.

It's a lot easier to study hidden things than it is to obey the obvious. It's harder to take small steps of obedience every day than it is to make a huge jump after seeing a vision in a sacred tortilla. It's easier to have a Precious Moments figurine speak than it is to read the Bible daily and discover who God really is.

God says I should love my wife and give myself to her. It's as plain as the Ephesians in my New Testament. The hard part is figuring out how to express that today, tangibly. Then again, maybe it's even harder to obey than figure it out.

"I heard you talking to someone," Andrea said. Then she looked at the shirt. "What are you going to do with that?"

"It's from college. Remember when I used to wear this?"

"Yes," she said. "I wanted to give it away a few years ago when you grew out of it. I was afraid you might get mad."

I held the shirt out to her as an offering. "It's not any good," I said. "Why don't you toss it for me. I have to get back to the laundry."

CHAPTER FORTY

It Only Takes Some Shoes to Get a Vacation Going

I bought a pair of sandals today. When you are expecting momentous things to happen, you want to have the right pair of shoes.

I'm not a sandal kind of guy, to be honest. There is something vulnerable about baring my pale feet in front of strangers and walking around all milky white until my skin turns the shade of lobster. But these are nice sandals, black with Velcro in three places—on the heel, over the top of the foot, and over the toe. They cost forty dollars, which is an unheard-of price in my world, but it was an impulse I couldn't resist. I could not bear telling my wife the amount.

"How much were they?" she asked.

"You don't want to know."

"Were they twenty-five dollars?" she said, wanting to shoot high so I could say, "Oh, not that much."

"More," I said.

"You're right, I don't want to know," she said.

So I took off my tennis shoes, kept my white socks on, and strapped myself into my forty-dollar pair of beachcombers. I did the dishes in my new sandals (which is not a new dance, I really did the dishes), getting the feel of them.

I snatched at little green peas gathered at the bottom of the sink. The water ran over them and they bounced on a soup-spoon like marionettes, mocking me. I remember thinking as a child about peas, wondering whether they liked being eaten or if they preferred being thrown in the trash or getting flushed down the drain. Since we do not have a disposal, I imagine there are hundreds of them under our sink, forgotten or mis-placed by dinners past. They are gathered in a great pea sea, congregating, enjoying their pea freedom.

See? I'm a grown man in dire need of a vacation!! I am imag-ining peas in the drain under my sink talking about revolution. William Wallace Pea is leading this band yelling, "Freedom!"

I told the kids about our South Carolina island destination. On the brochure there are people happily lying on the beach, no cares, no strain. I wonder how much they paid for their sandals. I wonder if they've ever had a pea fit like I'm having right now.

The water ran over a plate of burnt cheese, and I listened to someone on the radio read a story about his father. I wondered if my own father remembers when he used to hold me above his head, the waves crashing around us. I was scared back then, not because I couldn't swim, though that was true, but because I knew *he* couldn't swim. My mouth filled with salt water. I could hear him laughing below as he held my hands. Then another wave crashed into us, and I was on the edge of laughing to death or screaming all the air out of my lungs, and I just wanted to be on shore again near the seashells and the sand.

"Robert, you shouldn't do that," my mother would say when my father dragged me sputtering to shore.

"Oh, he liked it," my father replied. "We were just having fun, weren't we, Chris?"

I would nod, the salt water still fresh in my mouth. My father cannot hold me over his head now. He is older and much wiser. He also cannot afford the back surgery it would take if he even tried to lift one of my legs over his head. But there is some part of me that wishes he could lift me again, that I could go flying into the air in slow motion, turning back the hands of time to taste the joy and wonder of childhood.

My son joined me at the sink with the same haircut I had at his age, a buzz. He sucked on what we call a freeze pop, a sugary mass of ice that is fed though a thin plastic tube. We buy them by the truckload and put them in the freezer for hot days like this one. When I was a kid we had Fizzies, big tablets you'd drop in a glass of water that eventually turned into a horrid tasting drink no one with any sense would ingest. But because

163

they were fun to watch, we tolerated the taste. As my son anni-
hilated the freeze pop, I asked the great question before me.

"Bud?"

"Yeah, Dad."

"Do you think a pea would rather be eaten, thrown away,
or allowed to escape down the sink?"

He thought a minute then answered, "I don't like peas."

"I know. But if you were one, would you want to be eaten?"

He looked down, puzzled, like I had said something outside the scope of his abilities.

"Dad?"

"Yeah, Son."

"Are those new shoes?"

"Uh-huh, they're sandals."

"Cool."

"I never had sandals when I was a kid, at least that I can remember."

"How much did they cost?"

Why should a five-year-old care how much my sandals cost?
Have we warped him so much that this is now his first question?

"A lot," I said. "But I have really big feet and that makes
them cost more."

"Can I get some?"

"You already have some, don't you?"

164   "Yeah."

"Well, these are for me. For the island. You have to have the
right shoes when you go on vacation."

A breeze blew through the house, the wind bending the limbs of a birch outside. My hands stung from the hot soapy water, and the air felt fresh and clean on my face. A redbird hopped through the branches of a nearby tree until it reached the top.

"I think I would rather be eaten," my son said.

I had to think for a minute to remember our conversation.

"You mean you wouldn't want to escape and go with all the other free peas down the drain?"

"No. Peas were made to be eaten, I think."

"I think so too," I said.

The redbird flew away, frightened by a neighbor boy two years older than my son. He was without a shirt, and his shoulder blades stuck through his skin like cake servers.

"Can I go play with Casey?" my son asked.

"Yeah, go ahead."

He bounced into the living room toward his black tennis shoes, then the front door banged and he was gone.

The island is closer now that I have new sandals. It only takes something small to heighten the anticipation of something good. When I close my eyes I feel water, I taste the salt, and sense my father underneath me. My hands hold my son, who is laughing above me. One day we won't have to worry about peas and dishes and sunburns and herniated discs.

And then, far off in the distance, from somewhere otherworldly, I hear a still small voice call out to me.

"Were they thirty dollars?"

CHAPTER FORTY-ONE

——◆——

The Bible

While looking in my latest Christian catalog the other day I came upon an astounding thing. Ads for new Bibles. Hundreds of them. I'm not talking about different translations; I'm talking about specific Bibles for specific people.

The front page featured the *Life Application Bible* and the *Young Explorer's Bible*. A few pages farther, under the heading "Bargain Bibles," I found the following: *The Oswald Chambers Daily Devotional Bible, The Illustrated Family Time Bible, The Ryrie Study Bible, The New King James Mother's Love Bible, The Nelson Classic Wide Margin Center-Column Reference Bible, The Imperial Reference Bible, The Men's Devotional Bible, The Personal Growth Study Bible, The Wesley Bible, The MacArthur Study Bible, The Leadership Bible, The New Student Bible, The One-Minute Bible, The Full Life Study Bible,* and *The Adventure Bible*.

There was *The Giant Print Reference Bible, The Passages of Life Bible, The Spirit Filled Life Bible, The Wide Margin Study Bible* (which is published by the same people who bring you *The Wide Margin Center-Column Reference Bible*), *The Believer's Study Bible, The Thru the Year New Testament in Color, Charles Haddon Spurgeon's Devotional Bible, The Teen Study Bible, The NIV THIN-LINE Bible, The Quest Study Bible, The Senior's Devotional Bible, The New Living Translation Bible—Deluxe Text Edition, The Thompson Exhaustive Topical Bible, The New Oxford Annotated Bible, The Word in Life Study Bible, The Narrated Bible, The Youth Walk Devotional Bible, The Living Insights Study Bible,* and *The International Inductive Study Bible.*

But wait, there's more. I looked and behold, there was *The Open Bible* completely revised, *The New American Standard Loose-Leaf Daily Organizer Bible, The Everyday Study Bible, The HarperCollins Study Bible, The Experiencing God Study Bible, The Serendipity Bible, The King James Comfort Print Bible, The Hebrew-Greek Key Study Bible, The New Geneva Study Bible, The Prophecy Study Bible, The Life Application Red Letter Study Bible, The Complete Bible on Cassette, Alexander Scourby Holy Bible on Cassette,* and this doesn't even count *The Quiet Time Bible, The Online Bible, The HyperBible, The Adventures in Odyssey Bible, The Bible for Today's Christian Woman,* or my personal favorite, *The Bible in Pictures for Little Eyes.* I read the amplified version of that one.

I am grateful for access to so many versions and just about any imaginable reference material. I'm glad publishers want to get God's Word into the hands of people who need to read it, which is everybody.

As a matter of fact, I think the publishers have missed a few good titles. I've come up with *The Birth Order Bible, The Bible in Great Big Pictures for Nearsighted Little Eyes, The Chicken Soup Bible, The Slightly Overweight Women's Workout Bible, The Frank Peretti Scary Bible on CD*, and *The Left Behind Bible*. Perhaps by the time you read this, these will already be in publication.

I'm just perplexed by one thing. I read stories about people who have only scraps of the Bible, people who meet in dark places to hear God's Word read. The level of commitment in those places is astounding. These people give sacrificially and in some cases die for their faith. Then I look at the church in America and all the Bibles and materials on the Christian life available to it, and I wonder why it is so shallow. I wonder why I am so shallow.

There must be something missing. It must not be enough simply to own a Bible. The secret must not be in having good materials available. Perhaps, and I know this is a stretch, but maybe you have to be so committed, so sold out, that you actually open the thing and read it, and then do what it says.

It makes you wonder: With all the resources, what could happen in this country, in my town, on my corner, and in my home, if that would happen.

CHAPTER FORTY-TWO

———✦———

Empty Places Filled

Life without Jim has been hard. I realized that when we saw him last week. Jim is six years old and tall for his age. He has sandy hair and bright blue eyes, I think.

Before he moved at the end of the last school year, he played with my son Ryan. Ryan is a year and a half younger, but they got along well.

After kindergarten Jim would come over to our place. He and Ryan would play with Jim's cars or set up a McDonald's by our fireplace. They were good for about two hours together. Then they would fight, yell a couple of times, then make up.

I noticed a change in Ryan the first week after Jim moved. He didn't mope or hang his head, but there was something missing. Jim was missing.

A couple of days later the outburst came. Something was thrown, or someone was hit, and there was crying and wailing.

I remember my wife saying, "You miss Jim, don't you,

buddy?" Those are the times you thank God for a wife and not a spoon. Ryan nodded and buried his head in her chest. A few minutes later he was back to normal.

The summer went by and talk of Jim subsided. He was out there somewhere. Wisconsin was what they called it, but it was China for all my son knew. A four-hour drive is an eternity when you're four.

But a few weeks ago we heard Jim was coming for a visit. The excitement steadily built.

"When is Jim coming? Is it tomorrow? Can he come over?"

"Next week, bud, next week."

On the night I said, "Jim comes tomorrow," Ryan's eyes widened. He smiled and scrunched beneath the covers and shook with anticipation. It was one of those involuntary reactions that spreads to everyone in the room. I went to bed smiling, remembering my own childhood friend.

His name was Johnny, but we called him Little Johnny, because his older brother was also named John. Little Johnny came to our house, and we dug huge holes in the earth simply because we could. We stood on an old basketball backboard and pretended the hoop was the hatch to our spacecraft. If you fell off you would be lost forever with only enough oxygen to last five minutes. If your fellow astronaut didn't help you get back on quickly, you would swell up, turn blue, and eventually pop like a balloon. The search-and-rescue missions on that backboard were better than any film I've ever seen.

Somewhere in my elementary years Little Johnny moved.

I never heard from him again. His friendship left an empty hole in my life, with the memories piled up like dirt alongside the edges. I hadn't thought about Little Johnny for a long time, but Jim's return brought the memories back.

In the morning Ryan was up extra early wearing one of my long forgotten T-shirts that dusts the floor. After a bowl of cereal he was dressed and at the window.

"Remember, buddy," I said, "they're going to call after lunch for you to come over."

Questions persisted before and during lunch. I kept his coat off him as long as I could. We were about an hour away from Jim-down. The baby was asleep. Ryan had eaten lunch and cleaned his room. Barney was finished for the day. We sat and waited.

I got a cover and stretched out on the couch. He came with a couple of books, leaned against my chest, and we read *Hippo Lemonade*. When we got to the scary part, he drifted off. His breathing slowed, his eyes drooped, and soon we were both asleep.

The phone woke us and we both jumped. Jim was on his way. He would pick Ryan up at the corner, and they would walk back together, just like old times. We put our coats on and watched the street for any sign of him. It was a gray day and the street was wet. I heard an old muffler coming and soon a station wagon chugged by our house. When the smoke cleared I saw a blond head and some feet bouncing down the street.

"There he is!" Ryan said.

I crossed with him, and we waited a few inches past the street. Ryan wanted to walk as much sidewalk as he could with his friend. Jim was taller now, his shoulders wider. He cracked chewing gum and his cheeks were red from the cold.

"Hi, Jim," I said enthusiastically. "Boy it's been a long time since we've seen you. How are you doing?"

"Okay," he said softly. He looked at Ryan. "Are you ready?"

"Yeah."

Ryan's turtle tennis shoes scooted along the sidewalk, pushing at the leftover leaves. Hands in pockets. Head straight. No conversation.

They were nearly to the corner when Jim's head turned and he said something. Ryan looked up at him, his hair fluffy in the back, and laughed. They picked up the pace, heads bobbing. I would have given a fair amount of money to hear that conversation. To walk with them and listen to the musings of two friends. But there are some places you cannot go, and there are conversations you cannot hear. I crossed the street alone, and when I turned, they were running.

There are empty places where friends should be. We don't realize it until we find a friend to fill them. The sight of those two rounding the corner was enough to create my own hunger, to make me want to dig a hole or stand on an old backboard again. As I went back to the house, I think I saw the sun peek through the clouds.

---✦---

CHAPTER FORTY-THREE

My Noble Prize

Today I am sad because I have just learned I did not win the Nobel Prize for Literature. Again. This probably should not be surprising since I don't know anyone on the nominating committee. (These big prizes are all fixed, you know.)

Take the case of the 1998 winner, Portuguese novelist José Saramago, who is described as "an outspoken nonconformist who has a soft spot for the common man."

I, too, should have been considered for this prize, since I have a very big soft spot for the common man. To corroborate this, I refer you to the book *How to Measure Your Soft Spot for the Common Man* by French mathematician Hugo Yugo. I went through the ten steps he lists and have found my soft spot is absolutely *huge!* It's almost the size of Portugal. I demand consideration from the Swedish committee.

Saramago is also described as being "playful," having an

"exuberant imagination," and being one of Portugal's most popular contemporary writers.

I am unceasingly playful and possess an astoundingly exuberant imagination. If you do not believe this, ask anyone who has spent time in a dentist's waiting room with me. I am not one of Portugal's popular writers, but since the winner receives $978,000, I promise to reach out to the people of Portugal and become wildly popular by giving away tens and twenties to those who show up to adore me when I visit.

I also possess great compassion and irony. The Swedish Academy said Saramago was rewarded for these qualities and for his storytelling, which "continually enables us to apprehend an elusory reality."

You have no idea how long I've been trying to apprehend the elusory reality. Last summer I went on an elusory reality safari and managed to apprehend it, but, sadly, it got away before I could get it back to the car. In retrospect I should have killed it. This is tragic irony, therefore, that Saramago would win. I'm sure that was him in the Jeep behind me. He stole my escaped elusory reality, and now look where he is. That's not compassionate, but that's the kind of world we live in.

The parallels between my life and José Saramago's continue. José came from a poor family. I was born in West Virginia, one of the poorest states in the U.S. José never finished the university. I finished the university, but it didn't do me any good. José's first book sold badly. My first book sold very well but was really bad.

Through this yearly ordeal I have learned a valuable lesson. Some things in life are just not fair. Awards and rewards are fleeting. Think about it: If I had won the Nobel this year, I probably wouldn't have written this book. Talk about tragedy!

Perhaps today you are looking for the recognition you deserve. Perhaps you don't feel appreciated by the people you care most about. Perhaps your elusory reality has ear mites and needs a trip to the vet.

The apostle Paul had some good advice to a young man who may have been tempted by worldly pursuits. He wrote a letter to Timothy saying, "pursue righteousness, godliness, faith, love, endurance and gentleness. Fight the good fight of the faith. Take hold of the eternal life to which you were called...."

They don't give cash prizes for love. Faith is not an Olympic event. But those who pursue these goals in life will gain something of far greater value. It takes vision to make them your goal. How would your life change today if you did work hard for them?

The next time I hear someone has won a prestigious award, I'm going to be encouraged. I'm going to pursue gentleness instead of the Pulitzer. I'm going to run after godliness instead of an Academy Award. I'm going to set my affection on love instead of the Nobel Prize. And I have great hope in attaining each of these, because I happen to know someone on the heavenly committee.

CHAPTER FORTY-FOUR

Drive-Through Theology

D ad, how high is the sky?" my four-and-a-half-year-old son asked.

Being four and a half is a big deal to him these days. He let us know he doesn't like being called just "four." There's something about that half a year that makes him feel better. I tack it on when I can.

"Well," I said, "it's pretty high up there."

I didn't know whether he wanted a detailed answer on the upper atmosphere or if he was looking for a general response.

"I can see the moon," he said.

"Yeah, you know there are people who walked up there?"

"Really?" he said.

"Yeah. They went in a rocket, up through the clouds, and into space. You can go far into space."

"Is that infinity times?" he said.

He listens to his sisters talk about infinity. It's not an easy concept to grasp, but it has a certain ring to it. It rolls off the tongue well.

"Yes, you can probably go back into space an infinite amount of miles. You just keep going and going."

I thought he might ask about the Energizer Bunny next, but he looked puzzled. Something was stirring inside.

"Dad, do you have to go into space to see God?"

A profound question, I thought. He's been talking a lot about God lately, so I decided to give him a lesson in theology. I have heard about children making commitments to God at an early age, and I thought this might be his moment of reckoning.

"You don't have to go into space to know God," I said. "You can know him right here."

He frowned and shook his head and said, "I don't know Jesus."

"Would you like to?" I asked.

He nodded his head vigorously. We were just past Dairy Queen when I started the short catechism on holiness and sin.

"Do you know what sin is?" I said.

"No."

I proceeded to explain man's fallen nature and a scaled-back version of total depravity. We turned right past a car wash and a gas station. Then I said, "When you do bad things, it hurts God."

His face lit up. It seemed this might be the same look Saul had after the scales fell from his eyes. I was sure this was a golden moment of understanding. A breakthrough. I was looking for a place to pull over to commemorate this sacred occasion when my son looked into my face with his bright brown eyes.

He pointed to my left and yelled, "Look, Dad, Taco Bell!"

It's just SADD, I thought. *Spiritual Attention Deficit Disorder. It'll pass.* I tried to steer us back on track.

"Yeah. That's Taco Bell all right," I said, "but do you understand about sin?"

We came to a stoplight. He puckered his chin knowingly and waved off the question. His lack of knowledge had turned into a certain swagger.

"Dad," he said. "I know about Jesus now."

"You do?" I said. "And how do you know?"

He looked away from me and his eyes lit up again. He pointed to the right and yelled, "Look, Dad, Burger King!"

The theology lesson was over. I didn't push him further. Sometimes you have to know the difference between a holy moment and lunch.

CHAPTER FORTY-FIVE

God's Vacuum

The Bible stories we learn in Sunday school are so spectacular it's a bit depressing. David slays Goliath. The children of Israel walk around Jericho, and the walls fall down. Moses picks up a staff and turns it into a snake. And my personal favorite, Ehud, the left-handed Benjamite, kills fat King Eglon with a sword, and Eglon's belly folds over the handle of the knife. When I get to heaven, I'm going to find whoever recorded that Eglon story and thank them.

These huge biblical events yield great lessons, but things like this never happen to me. The biggest giant I've slain in the last year is the skunk in our backyard, and I got rid of him with ammonia and some moth balls, not a slingshot. (He didn't perish, by the way, he just moved.)

We emphasize the miracles of Jesus and the way they showed his authority. We teach of his death and resurrection, for these are the hinge points of our faith. Without Jesus' miracles and rising from the dead, Christians have nothing.

But there are many wonderful stories in the Bible about normal, ordinary people going about their duties and finding God. Compare your everyday life to two brothers working by the Sea of Galilee. They were minding their own business, casting their net into the lake and hoping for fish. Their hands were callused from years of hard work.

"You really ought to wash your clothes more often," Andrew says. "They've lost that sparkle."

"Hey," Simon replies, "I'm a fisherman. I'm supposed to smell like fish. If you want sparkle, become a tailor."

"Hand me the other net, will you?" Andrew says. As he turns he notices someone behind them. "Hey Simon, I think we're being watched."

Simon picks up the net and glances at another ordinary-looking man standing by the shore. He's much like them, only dryer. "Doesn't look like a fisherman," Simon says. "I wonder what he wants?"

If it were me, I would not have been down by the water looking for followers. The social elite don't make their living fishing. You find common people at the shore. If it were me looking for disciples, I would have first chosen a terrific singer who could bring in the crowds. Then I would have looked for someone with a reputation in the political establishment. Choosing followers is a strategic matter. You can't waste these choices. As a matter of fact, I probably would have hired an agent and made an infomercial to get things started.

Jesus did the exact opposite. He chose two fishermen. He even did it in an ordinary way. I would have made a great motivational speech with flip charts. I would have identified their felt needs. Jesus didn't wow. He simply said, "Come, follow me, and I will make you fishers of men."

After calling these two brothers, which from a human perspective was probably not a great move because of all the fighting brothers do, he called two more fishermen brothers.

"James, John, where do you two think you're going?" Zebedee must have said. "Come back here! We have work to do!"

All their father had left that day was hired men and a vision of his sons walking away with this strange bunch—just everyday workers, minding their own business, who were changed by an encounter with Jesus.

Again, if it were me trying to build a base of moral people to call my disciples, I would have looked in the ranks of the religious. You don't want people of the world, like tax collectors, following you. But that's exactly who Jesus picked.

"As he walked along, he saw Levi son of Alphaeus sitting at the tax collector's booth. 'Follow me,' Jesus told him, and Levi got up and followed him."

"Whoa, wait a minute, Jesus," the others must have thought. "You don't understand. A tax collector is even lower

181

than a fisherman. These are not the kind of people to hang around with." To make things worse, Jesus goes to Levi's house and has dinner with him and his friends. He has gone from the common to big-time sinners! Everyday people, riotous sinners, breaking bread with the King of Glory.

God seems to get a kick out of interrupting the lives of people like you and me. When he has really good news he sends a choir of angels to a handful of shepherds on a hillside. He takes joy in the prospect of changing the life of someone like the woman at the well. She was there to draw water, which is just about as mundane a task as you can imagine, with the possible exception of changing diapers. She was a Samaritan, a person a good Jew would not even acknowledge, let alone speak to. But Jesus does speak to her and asks for a drink.

Their conversation is amazing. Jesus tells her about living water and reveals the depth of her sin. She rightly recognizes him as a prophet. Then Jesus does something incredible. In the middle of nowhere he reveals his true identity to this adulterous woman.

The woman said, "I know that the Messiah is coming. When he comes, he will explain everything to us."

Then Jesus declared, "I who speak to you am he" (see John 4:7-26).

As far as I can tell, the only prerequisite to entering a relationship with Christ is to be thirsty for living water and be willing to recognize you're a sinner. I think that covers just about everyone.

Before anyone says to me, "Hey, I'd be glad to have that experience by my washing machine today," I can guarantee these same scenes will not happen to you. Jesus chose his first disciples in the first century. There can only be one woman at the well. There was only one person in the crowd chosen to help him carry his cross. But you and I have an opportunity to live out another scene of mundane grace today, one that can be equally exciting.

Paul, who could have called his previous business "Persecutions Я Us," wrote a letter to the Colossians and said these words: "Whatever you do, work at it with all your heart, as working for the Lord, not for men, since you know that you will receive an inheritance from the Lord as a reward. It is the Lord Christ you are serving" (Colossians 3:23-24).

For those who recognize their sin and accept God's forgiveness, there is wonderful news. Whatever you do today can be a holy project. It could be casting a net for fish or filling your tank at the corner gas station. It could be fighting traffic or having your car tested for emissions. It could be making dinner, doing laundry, going to the library, paying bills, digging a sewer line, raking leaves, or slicing bologna. God says to do whatever you do with all your heart today, and do it for him. You're not doing the task so you can have time for God; instead, you accomplish that task for his glory, with his blessing. That view of daily duties keeps complaints down, truancy low, and doesn't need a coffee break every half-hour!

When I know I'm not just working for an employer but am

doing my job for God, my attitude and my level of performance change. If you believed you were drawing water for the God who made you, you would probably do it a little differently. If you knew Jesus would show up today as you watch your children, you probably wouldn't stick them in front of the television.

The truth is, today is not just for me. My vacuum cleaner is really God's vacuum.

I will now tell you how far short I have fallen with this principle. I'm not proud of this little slice of my life. Not ten minutes after I wrote the words above about the vacuum—and I am not making this up—I went into the living room where Andrea was getting the little ones ready for her women's meeting.

"I'm going to put you in the car and come back in here and vacuum," she said, the Rice Chex and popcorn still fresh from the night before. "That is, unless your father wants to run the vacuum."

I rolled my eyes and thought of all the important things I needed to do, then thought how silly it is to put children in a cold car and come inside to clean the floor.

"I guess I'll do it if it'll make you feel better," I said.

I went downstairs for something and in a few minutes heard the sound of the vacuum. I waited until she had enough time to finish, then came bounding cheerily back into the room.

"Hey, I told you I'd do that for you," I said, acting a little hurt.

"I know, but it didn't seem like you really wanted to. I decided to go ahead and do it rather than feel guilty."

I tried doing the listener-speaker technique that Gary Smalley talks about. "I hear you saying I made you feel guilty by the way I said I'd do it."

"That's right."

"I'm sorry."

With that she was out the door and smiling, but I realized I had missed a great opportunity. That *was* God's vacuum. That was my opportunity to draw water from the well. Instead, I dropped my net and ran.

There will be other opportunities for me to work with all my heart today. If I can be faithful and jubilant in these things, I won't have a problem slaying giants or shouting down the walls. Who knows? If I'm really faithful, maybe I'll get to play swords with a fat king someday!

CHAPTER FORTY-SIX

———◆———

O for a Thousand Necks

My son's neck is perfect. It is just big enough to get my
thumb and index finger halfway around. This is better
than a leash. When we're walking across the street I don't have
to hold his hand, which he doesn't seem to like anymore. I
guide him with one strong hand around the neck. This is called
security.

You can judge a person's character by their neck. There is
strength and purpose there. Unlike the corner of a person's
mouth, the neck never drools on your pillow during Sunday afternoon naps. The neck will not say bad things about you behind your back or make faces at you. The neck is the body's
barometer.

You can sense a person's openness by their reaction when
you grab their neck. Some recoil and shake you off. Others

tense and allow you to hold them, but you can tell they want no part of it.

It's no wonder the Bible refers to someone against the purposes of God as "stiff-necked." Straight and rigid are the necks of those who shun God's directives.

I thought of all this one Sunday morning as I stood beside my son in worship. He had asked to see the church bulletin in advance that morning, not having one of his own. He took it and read the verse fragment at the top from Hebrews, his mouth moving with each word, "let us draw near to God with a sincere heart in full assurance of faith." Then he scanned the songs and choruses printed underneath.

He reads well for his age, but not at the same singing speed as the adults. The week before, I had opened his eyes to the wonders of hymn texts and how the verses are read. He needed a bit of time to prepare, so I watched him as he sounded out the sentences.

We stood for the first worship song, and I placed my hand on his shoulder, just able to reach it. I saw him down there, head bowed, lips barely moving as the music enveloped us. I could not hear his voice, and if I had stooped to his level I believe he would have stopped.

I instinctively slipped my hand onto his neck, touching it softly from behind. I could feel his character in my left hand, along with his carotid pulse, and then something even more wonderful. I felt the vibration of his praise. It rattled between my fingers and slipped into the room unnoticed, like a mouse sniffing in the corner of a darkened hallway. Nevertheless, it was there, and I held it for the first time.

I wondered if God could give me such a neck, full of character, limber and not stiff. Could he make my praise as pure and innocent as my son's? I did not feel a cosmic hand slip onto my own neck. I believe it was there all along.

CHAPTER FORTY-SEVEN

The Island of ME

I once read a book that chronicled the incredible journey of a man who quit his lucrative job, divorced his wife, sold his possessions, and moved to a beach house along the coast of California. It was a beautifully written book with a nice cover that made you want to do the same.

In those pages I sensed a searching, the same desire I have to salve the daily ache of the ordinary. The author was trying to fill the hole in his soul with sand, salt air, and driftwood art. But a beautifully written book does not make it a true book, nor does emptying ourselves of all responsibility help us achieve authenticity.

Going back to nature, getting close to crabs and mackerel, will not, in the end, prove your existence is worthy. It only gets you closer to crabs and mackerel. It's easier for me to see this flaw since I'm not sure crabs and mackerel are that fond of people like me. I would rather eat them than spend time with

189

them. But something in me yearns for this kind of romance. It sounds fulfilling to leave everything and everyone behind and begin again.

Upon closer examination of the story, however, I saw it was not a life filled with simple abundance. It was simply pathetic.

The author of this beautifully written book pointed to Paul Gauguin as an authentic, artistic individual. To correctly pronounce the French name Gauguin, you must sound as if you have a big hunk of crab in your mouth. Paul Gauguin forsook his wife and five children and took a residence in Tahiti, where he could paint all day and smell the sea and live as if nothing else in the world mattered but his gift. Perhaps if I were more gifted, like Gauguin, I would understand his choice. This, I believe, is one of the blessings of mediocrity.

Anyone can run away from life. Anyone can take off their watch and say they are free from the restrictions of time. As idyllic as it sounds, I have decided not to emulate these people. I want to be a man who takes off his watch and sits in the middle of the floor, no matter how crowded with toys and stale Cheerios, and plays with his children until they believe he truly loves them. I want to be a man who is not concerned about getting away from every encumbrance of life but who wants to use those encumbrances to make a statement to those around him: "You are more important to me than things. You are more important than my ambitions. You are eternal. These are temporal. I want to spend my life on you, not on them or even myself."

As I look at God's supreme example of authenticity, Jesus, my true desire is to be like him. He was patient. His words were healing. He was empty of all but love. He was without any puff or pretense.

But amid this grand desire, I have a desperate problem: I am no better than the person who runs off to Tahiti and abandons his children, for every day I am just as selfish. I don't often take off my watch and let the children jump on my back, but when I do, I'm only down there a few minutes before I look at the clock and wonder when I can start doing what I really want.

Every day with little decisions I choose the island of ME instead of some exotic solace. It looks a lot more respectable than Tahiti, but it seems just as far away to my wife and kids. The only difference between Gauguin and me, other than the way you pronounce it, is that I am left with a thousand choices each day instead of one big one.

I don't need an island. This place is where I want to be, with my feet firmly planted between these people, just below a sign that says "Grace."

CHAPTER FORTY-EIGHT

Faith = Two Wheels and Kneepads

I took my son to the backyard, away from the crowds and the nice sidewalk in front, to learn a difficult lesson. We were not going to the woodshed; we were headed toward a grassy knoll with his bike. He was self-conscious about not being able to ride it.

"Why did you take the wheels off?" he asked, as if I were Abraham.

"We are going to sacrifice—I mean, we are going to learn how to ride a bike today." I said this with great confidence. "By the end of today, you will be riding this bike."

His jaw dropped. He didn't know whether to believe me or laugh.

"There's nothing but grass back here," he said.

"Trust me."

"But—"

"Trust me."

I always find it difficult to explain myself to my children when I have really good ideas. When I have wonderful things planned, like a surprise trip to the park or to a movie, I want them to show equal anticipation even though they don't know what's going to happen. I had a forward view. In my mind I saw the look on his face when he finally took control, when he pedaled and realized he was actually riding. I could already see how grateful he'd be that I'd taught him.

"Dad, I don't want to do this."

"Sure you do. It'll be fun. Get on."

"Dad, really. Can we go back in front and you hold the back of the seat while I pedal?"

"No. You're going to do it by yourself. You're going to ride this bike. Today. Believe."

We were perched on top of a small hill that gently slopes about six feet. His toes touched the grass as he rocked back and forth, alternating feet. He kept glancing behind us, as if an angel would suddenly stop the whole proceeding and produce a ram from a thicket to ride the bike for him.

"I don't think I want to do this," he said.

"You'll be fine. This is the way I learned. You just put your feet on the pedals, and I'll push you."

"No."

"Really, you'll be fine. Don't worry about pedaling, just keep your balance until you get to the bottom."

"Dad—"

"Trust me."

I really did learn to ride a bike this way. I rode down our front yard and coasted on the lush, green grass over the septic tank. It was my first experience of "feeling" the bike, of knowing I was guiding it and not the other way around. So I had no trouble giving my son a little push that day.

He wobbled the handlebars the first few feet, then, as he was nearing the bottom, everything fell apart. *Whomp!* I ran and helped him to his feet, but it was clear his future counselor will make a killing on the "trust issues" that arise from that day.

"Come on," I coaxed, "one more time and you'll see. You'll be riding in no time."

He ran inside the house crying. I was left holding his helmet and a bike much too small for my frame. *Maybe it's something you have to do for yourself,* I thought. After all, I was alone when I finally got it, when my bike and I became one. Maybe it has to be his idea.

The next day passed without the usual question. He didn't want help. He didn't even seem interested. A neighbor stopped and expressed concern: "He was over at the house yesterday, and I asked if he wanted to go for a bike ride with us."

194   "Uh-oh," I said.

"Yeah. He just hung his head and told me he couldn't ride yet. I felt sorry for him."

"He'll get it," I said without a hint of nervousness. Then I wondered if he would. What happens if he never learns to ride his bike? What will people think? Will anyone ever buy a book from a man who can't teach his own son how to ride a two-wheeler? Oh the shame!

Wait. My literary career is not a good reason for him to learn to ride a bike.

There's something about riding a bike that transcends all parental wishes. A child has to want to ride. He has to taste the wind in his face and the feeling of the road rushing under two wheels. He has to want his best friend by his side as they head for the ice-cream shop, standing up for the potholes and jumping mud puddles. That's what draws kids to bikes, not parents shoving them down a hill.

However, there's a cost to the ride. You have to pay the price in order to enjoy that scene. You have to fall and get up and fall again and get up and fall and put a bandage on your elbow and fall again. Learning to ride is a risk every time you pick both feet off the ground and put your trust in two tires and your own sense of balance. Until you're ready to go through the pain, you're not really ready.

Riding a bike is a lot like life. You can play it safe and not get involved, or you can put both feet on and try. Life is a risk. If you stuff your talent and desires in a box along with your dreams, you'll survive. But you'll also never know what God could do with you. Living fully is a daily choice at Mundane and Grace.

A few days later, I walked to the elementary school nearby. The sun made the grass glow. I glanced up the long sidewalk and saw my son cautiously riding toward me. He had lots of bruises and a few scars by then, but I didn't notice them. All I could see was his smile.

CHAPTER FORTY-NINE

Daydream Believing

S ometimes I see my life as a film inside my head, complete with stereo soundtrack. It's easier than living the real thing, this vision without celluloid. Sometimes I close my eyes and hear the music and sound effects, but a few minutes later a jet passes overhead and our dog barks, and it makes me want to roll up my newspaper and scold the world into its cage.

When I was in school they called this daydreaming. They said I was goofing off. But even now, in the middle of my life, it's not a bad exercise.

Full shot of the exterior. Shadow overtakes a man sitting on the front steps of his home. Sound effects—lone bird in tree, soft wind whistling.

FRIEND: I thought I'd find you here. Mind if I sit down?
ME: Please. I'm glad for the company.

Porch swing creaks.

FRIEND: Sure is pretty. I love this corner.

ME: Yeah, I take it for granted most of the time.

FRIEND: Easy to do. Everything's going so fast, it's crazy.

Car passes nearby. Emotional music score sneaks underneath dialog.

FRIEND (continued): What question are you trying to answer with that book?

ME: I don't really have a question.

FRIEND: 'Course you do. Everybody's got a question they're trying to answer. Life is a series of questions.

ME: You're sounding like Oprah.

FRIEND: Don't mean to.

ME: I guess…I wonder what good I'm doing. Why am I here instead of some other corner in some other part of the world? Should I just be content with the ambiguity?

FRIEND: Big word.

ME: It comes from a quote by Gilda Radner that I wanted to put in the book.

FRIEND: Is she a theologian?

ME: No, a comedian. She died of ovarian cancer.

FRIEND: Shame. Why didn't you include the quote?

198 ME: Couldn't find the right place. Didn't fit.

FRIEND: What did she say?

Music stops abruptly.

EDITOR: Oh no, you're not getting it in that way. No fair!

FRIEND: Who's she?

ME: My editor. She's nice, except when she has a red pen in her hand.

FRIEND (compassionately): Come on, Editor, let him put the quote in.

EDITOR: No! I'm not even sure this whole chapter fits. It's a different tone, a different layout. We might need to cut the whole thing.

FRIEND: Let him do it, and you can cut it if you don't like it, okay?

EDITOR: Oh, all right. But just this once.

A train whistles and both look to the right. Music swells again.

ME: Gilda said, "I wanted a perfect ending. Now I've learned, the hard way, that some poems don't rhyme, and some stories don't have a clear beginning, middle and end. Like my life, this book is about not knowing, having to change, taking the moment and making the best of it, without knowing what's going to happen next. Delicious ambiguity."[1]

FRIEND: That's good. What does it mean?

ME: I think she was answering my question. I treat the uncertainties of life as my enemy. But maybe they're the best part. Ambiguity is like the vegetable part of the meal. Too often we try to push it out of the way or smother it in butter.

FRIEND: But what about your faith? Isn't that a certainty?

ME: My faith is the one thing that isn't uncertain, because it's based on someone who doesn't change.

FRIEND: There are so many people who don't know that certainty. You might be the one to tell them.

Wide shot of yard. Man comes to white fence at the edge of the yard.

NEIGHBOR: Hey! You're not gonna give me that Bible stuff now, are you? I mean, it was really interesting up to this point.

ME: No. I'm not going to shove it down your throat, if that's what you mean.

NEIGHBOR: You Christians. You think you have all the answers.

ME: No, that's the point. We don't have the answers, but we do know the one who does.

EDITOR: That was trite.

FRIEND: I have to agree.

ME: Okay. No, Christians don't have all the answers. And if I've acted that way toward you, I'm sorry. Really sorry.

NEIGHBOR: You are?

ME: Yeah. The last thing I want to do is act like some know-it-all jerk. I want to be your friend.

NEIGHBOR: Okay, we're friends. I bet I have to convert or stop smoking now, right?

ME: No. I'll still be your friend if you smoke, and I'll try to be the best one you've ever had. But I won't stop talking about what's important.

There is an uncomfortable pause as all four stare at each other.

EDITOR: Shouldn't there be some kind of closure to the relationship?
FRIEND: Don't you see? That's the ambiguity.
EDITOR: Oh. Sorry.
ME: This still doesn't answer the question of why I'm here though.

Long shot from top of tree looking down on yard. Young child runs into yard with back to camera, a football in his hand.

CHILD: Daddy, can you teach me to throw one of these?
FRIEND: I think I gotta be goin'.
ME: No, stay.
EDITOR: Me too.
ME: You ought to watch. Might do you good.
NEIGHBOR: Hey, mind if I bring my kid over? We can play two on two.

A dog barks. A jet passes overhead. Fade to black.

[1] Gilda Radner, *It's Always Something* (Sydney: Simon & Schuster, 1989), 268.

CHAPTER FIFTY

Living Backwards

Kierkegaard was a famous theologian whose name, on a good day, I can spell. I don't know much of what he said and probably wouldn't agree if I could understand it, but he did say something profound about life. Get ready, here comes a quote your friends will want to put on their refrigerator:

The trouble with life is that we understand it backwards, but we have to live it forwards.

I told you it was magnet worthy.

This concept intrigues me. Every day I get a little wiser about life, love, parenting, and cutting the lawn with an electric mower. I learn something new about the brevity of time, the preciousness of babies, and how to drive in snow without using too much windshield-wiper fluid.

Sadly, I needed that wisdom a decade ago with problem

202

areas such as communication and plumbing. My wife has taught me great things about communication. Had I known them years ago, we could have avoided much painful conflict. I'm still working on the plumbing.

For example, one Saturday evening Andrea became snippy with me. After sixteen years together, I realize she is only snippy when she is upset with me or when they're out of organic apple juice at the whole-foods store. As we walked our normal route that evening, I felt intuitively it had nothing to do with apple juice and everything to do with the fact that I had worked late Friday night and had an all-day Saturday assignment away from home. It was nothing unexpected. We both knew in advance I had these duties, but when Saturday evening came I was in the presence of Queen Snippy.

"What's the matter?" I asked, feeling not so intuitive.

"Mugwumarumpagum," she mumbled.

"What was that?"

"Mmmuwhurumagumpalamadamadingdong."

"I can't hear you when you mumble, now turn around here and—"

"Do you know," she interrupted, "what I've been through the past two days?"

Suddenly her powers of enunciation were intact! Queen Snippy was off her throne and onto my back.

"Do you know how hard it is to have seven children and take care of them all week and then come to Saturday and find you have to do it all by yourself?"

I know it is hard because every now and then I actually take care of two or three. Andrea is still breastfeeding Reagan, and he is no longer the cute toddler but is more like a cute bulldozer that won't run out of gas. Andrea now affectionately calls him Beast Boy.

Sixteen years ago I would have gotten defensive at her harangue. I would have tried to compete with her. "Okay," I would have said, "I'll breastfeed that baby all next week, and we'll see who complains about it!" Or I would have said the much more dastardly words, "You were the one who wanted a big family! You were the one who decided to have all these—"

WHACK!

That's what it would have sounded like a few years ago. But as I listened to Andrea talk and tried to fight back those defensive feelings, I understood she just needed a little verbal affirmation. It was a great struggle not to harangue back, because I can harangue with the best of them.

A few blocks went by without words. I got up my nerve and said something very foreign, very uncomfortable.

"Say, I was gone last night and most of today. I bet that was pretty hard having all the kids, huh?"

She looked shocked at first, then smiled, then put her arm around me. She knew I understood. It was all she needed.

Why do we have to go into marriage not knowing defusing sentences like this? Why are we forced to live forwards? Why can't we become parents when we're fifty and let the kids be their own grandparents? Why do the career-striving years have to be the ones when the kids need you at their band concert? Why are the pipes under the sink dripping?

The answer to these questions, excluding profound plumbing problems, is not found in reducing our stress levels or waiting until we're one hundred to have an Isaac. The answer is to reverse our lives right where we are. We need to live backwards.

Living backwards is the process by which we take today's experiences and view them through the prism of eternity. (Hey, that sentence might go well on the back of the bathroom door.) Living backwards is the principle my father grasped when he would say, "A hundred years from now you'll never know it." Living backwards is a set of daily choices, mostly mental, that take us outside our pettiness and give a new perspective.

Andrea loves working on Creative Memories scrapbooks. She sits for hours and cuts up perfectly good pictures so she can tape them in albums and put stickers and borders around the pages. It is fatiguing to watch, but she enjoys it immensely and has quite a collection of photo books for each of the children.

She had been working for nearly two hours on two pages, cutting, recutting, taping, bordering, sanding, welding, etc., when the laundry called. Upon returning to the room, she found Beast Boy on the floor with a colored marker. His whole left hand was green, and he had also slashed splotches of green all over her wonderful pages and pictures. She wanted to yell

205

and scream. She wanted to lament her long labor on this project. But as she walked in, he put his hand in the air and proudly said, "Look, Mom! Geen."

Instead of lecturing or spanking, instead of tearing up her hard work and throwing it away, Andrea pulled out her camera and took a photo of Beast Boy holding up his hand and sitting by her ruined pages. She put that picture in the corner of one page and left the green markings all around as a tangible reminder of how things used to be. She turned a ruined page into a masterpiece. It is a memory she will treasure the rest of her life.

If she had been living forwards at that moment, she would have punished him for such nasty behavior. But because she lived backwards, because she realized this was not a malicious event but a playful one, she chose a better way.

How can you live backwards today? It's a simple process. Whatever frustration you're confronting, at work or at home, picture yourself at seventy-five, sitting in a rocking chair beside your spouse. Then ask yourself, "What's the best thing to do right now? What can I do today that will make me happiest when I'm old and gray and I have nothing left but my gums and my memories?"

Let's not stop here. Go further with the concept and answer these questions: How much would it take to be happy with where you are financially? How much would it take to be able to say, "I'm satisfied with my possessions; I'm not going to spend more time trying to make money and accumulate more things?"

In the deeper aspects of your life, how much does it take for you to be satisfied with your relationship with your spouse and children? How much does it take for you to be satisfied with God?

When I analyze myself, I find I'm pretty happy with the time I spend with my wife and children. Sure, I could do better, but all in all, I feel okay about it. It's the same with God. He gets Sunday mornings and a few devotional moments throughout the week, if I have the time. I could do better, but I'm okay.

I think this way because I have become a forwards-world person who puts great value on things that don't last. In the process, I automatically forfeit things that really matter. Daily, I'm failing the rocking-chair test.

The saddest part of this equation is that I'm sacrificing true satisfaction for an illusion. What could be more fulfilling than close relationships with my family and with the one true God? What could possibly bring more satisfaction than investing in the lives of other people? I'm not only cheating my family when I put a priority on work or my ambitions, I cheat myself.

I've decided, as I sit on the front porch and watch the kids play on the front lawn, I'm going to settle for more in my life. I don't have time to settle for less. And if others look at my lifestyle and call me backwards, I'll just smile and say, "Exactly!"

—◆—

The Bartimaeus Principle

I leave you with a final thought from columnist and author Bob Greene. I've talked with him a few times about issues he's covered and books he's written. One of his *Chicago Tribune* columns described a scene at the Newark airport. The parents of a severely retarded young woman stood near a long line of people as their daughter inched toward the check-in. It was a big moment for them. She was changing her ticket all by herself. Maybe it was the first time she had ever done something like this.

"I've always thought most columnists read like they're either in Washington sitting back sucking on a pipe and thinking great thoughts about the M-X missile debate in Congress," Greene said, "or it sounds like their editor has assigned them something. To me, it's always best if it sounds like you've gotten home at the end of the day, called your best friend on the phone, and said, 'You won't believe who I met today. You won't believe what I saw today.'"

I asked him about the scene at the airport, watching the mother and father from the end of the line.

"I wrote that piece because the pride on her parents' faces and the pride in her own face were the best things I saw that day," he said.

"But most people wouldn't see that," I said. "Most people in line behind her would be upset about having to wait. They're thinking, why doesn't someone do something?"

Greene nodded and looked down at the table. He had seen those reactions to the young woman as well.

"Why did everybody else miss it?" I said. "Why did you see it?"

"I don't know," he said. "I guess you gotta look."

That's pretty good advice for anyone's journey. It's what I call the Bartimaeus principle. Blind Bartimaeus was sitting by the side of the road, begging, as Jesus walked by. Bartimaeus shouted and kept shouting until Jesus beckoned.

"What do you want me to do for you?" Jesus said.

Bartimaeus replied, "Rabbi, I want to see."

The prayer was answered. Immediately Bartimaeus received his sight, and he used it to follow Jesus along the road.

I feel like Bartimaeus today. There is so much I haven't seen about myself and those around me. I haven't seen the good gifts God has given at the bottom of the laundry hamper, at the top of the full vacuum bag. At the end of the day when it has taken my last ounce of strength to pull the covers over my shoulders, when I wonder where God is in the details of life, I lift a short prayer that echoes down the Jericho road.

O God, I want to see.